Cycling Along the Canals of New York State

*Scenic Rides on the Historic Waterways
of the Empire State*

Cycling Along the Canals of New York State

Scenic Rides on the Historic Waterways of the Empire State

Louis Rossi

Second Edition

VITESSE PRESS

Montpelier, Vermont

Cycling Along the Canals of New York State

Published by Vitesse Press

917.471

PMB 367, 45 State Street

ROS

Montpelier, VT 05601-2100

www.vitessepress.com

Copyright @ 2006 by Vitesse Press

Library of Congress Cataloging-in-Publication Data

Rossi, Louis.
  Cycling along the canals of New York State : scenic rides on the historic waterways of the Empire State / Louis Rossi.-- 2nd ed.
    p. cm.
  Rev ed of: Cycling along the canals of New York. c1999.
  ISBN 0-941950-39-5
  1. New York (State)–Guidebooks. 2. Canals–New York (State)–Guidebooks. 3. Trails--New York (State)–Guidebooks. 4. Cycling–New York (State)–Guidebooks. I. Rossi, Louis. Cycling along the canals of New York. II. Title.
  F117.3.R68 2006
  917.47'1044--dc22
                    2005035360

Design and layout by RavenMark, Inc.
Manufactured in the United States of America

10 9 8 7 6 5 4 3 2 1

Distributed in the United States by Alan C. Hood, Inc. (717-267-0867)

For sales inquiries and special prices for bulk quantities, contact Vitesse Press at 802-229-4243 or write to the address above.

About the Author

Louis Rossi has lived along the canals of New York for most of his life. For three decades, he worked as a civil engineer for the New York State Department of Transportation, which owned and operated these historic canals. He was involved in many important decisions affecting their future and became intimately familiar with the canal communities as well as the people running the canals.

Rossi is active as a recreational cyclist and bike racer. He is a licensed USCF racing coach and coaches a youth racing team. He has bicycled extensively in North America and in England, Switzerland and Italy.

Rossi notes that the canal region of New York, with its wonderful scenery, excellent roads and trails, and important history, is unparalleled for cycling. He rode several thousand miles in preparing this book.

Contents

Introduction

*This book is a complete guide to nearly one thousand miles of the
historic canals of New York. It is also an invitation to immerse
yourself in the rich history of the last four centuries and the
American Indian culture that preceded the arrival of Europeans.
You will see how geography, which facilitated water level or
river-based transportation, fostered the creation of the powerful
Iroquois Confederacy. You will also come to understand how the
waterways enabled the Dutch, British, and American commerce of
the region to expand, turning the colony of New York, as
George Washington suggested, into "the Empire State."
So get ready to relive early American history as you cycle through
some of the most scenic countryside in the Northeast.*

Upstate New York is filled with both fascinating scenery and
history and there's no better way to see it than from a bicycle.
Many visitors to the area are surprised to learn that the Erie
Canal survives and is still in operation. But, when you take several
of the rides in this book, you'll find that not only does the Erie Canal
survive, it flourishes. You'll find that three other operating canals —
Champlain, Oswego, and Cayuga-Seneca, are part of the system and that
there are also many historic canal routes which make wonderful bike
ventures. You'll ride alongside many of these canals on wonderful trails,
including the nationally acclaimed Canalway Trail along the Erie Canal.

Here are some of the highlights this guidebook will help you find
by bicycle or by boat.

- The highest flight of lift locks in the world
  - ~ Old Erie Canal Locks 4, 9-18 in Albany County
  - ~ Erie Barge Canal Locks 2-6 in Saratoga County
- The historic homes of the Johnson Family

- Haudenosaunee History (Five Nations and Six Nations; the Iroquois)
  - ~ Ossernenon, Shako:Wi Center, Ganondagan and more
- Schoharie Crossing State Park
  - ~ Schoharie Aqueduct, Yankee Locks and Putnam's Store
- The story of General Herkimer
  - ~ Herkimer Home
  - ~ Oriskany Battlefield
- At Little Falls:
  - ~ Ruins of the 17th Century Western Inland Navigation Company's Canal
  - ~ The highest single lift-lock in the Americas
  - ~ Giant glacial potholes
- Old Erie Canal State Park
- Erie Canal Museum in the Weighlock Building in Syracuse
- The Great Embankment and Genesee Aqueduct at Rochester
- The Lockport Flight of Locks and the Great Cut
- "Lost" feeder canals including:
  - ~ The Chenango Canal — most scenic summit-level
  - ~ The Black River Canal — toughest climb
  - ~ The Genesee Canal — most awesome gorge, the Grand Canyon of New York

  Crooked Lake Canal — great interpretative historic signage
- "Living" feeder canals:
  - ~ Oswego Canal
  - ~ Cayuga-Seneca Canal
  - ~ The genesis of Woman's Rights movement in Seneca Falls
  - ~ Guide to the canals of the Finger Lakes
- Champlain Canal — great scenic beauty and remarkable history

The key to building all the canals of New York was a glacial gap, the passageway of the Hudson River through the Hudson Highlands about thirty miles north of New York City. Here, constant glacial activity over almost 20,000 years carved a salt-water sea-level passageway through the Appalachian Mountain Chain. This passageway is unique in North America. It is one of the few fjords in North America and was the natural feature that made the Erie Canal possible. In fact, the entire Erie Canal route, from Albany to Buffalo, lies west of the Appalachian Mountains.

Because of this glaciation, water transportation was relatively easy. There were no mountains to climb; small boats and canoes could go almost anywhere. The Indians let the impenetrable forests define the boundaries of their territories, more or less content to use the waterways to define their

Cyclists can ride along nearly 1000 miles of historic canals in upstate New York.

nations. However, when these forests became the unmarked border between French Canada and English America, border disputes began. New York's waterways, used for centuries by Native Americans, became the route of warfare. As a result, as you bike along the canals of New York, you will pass historic sites from the French and Indian War, the Revolutionary War, and the War of 1812 — in many ways all one conflict that lasted nearly 200 years.

It began in the late 1600s with a series of wars known collectively as the French and Indian Wars. They took place along the vague boundaries between the French settlements along the Saint Lawrence River in Canada and the British colonies along the Atlantic. To a great extent, this involved the Upper Hudson River, Mohawk River, and Lake Champlain regions. The cost of winning these wars, imposed upon the colonies by Great Britain, was a principal cause of the American Revolution. Much of the Revolution, particularly events leading up to the decisive battles of Oriskany and Saratoga, also took place across the Hudson, Mohawk,

The Erie Canal and all the other canals that joined it were powered by horse or mule teams that towed wooden freight and passenger boats at about 4 mph. Every canal had a single towpath along one side. It is this towpath that is now the recreational off-road bike path (locally known by many names but most often called the Canalway Trail) that you will often bicycle atop when you visit these historic alignments.

Jim Cassatt

You can charter a canal boat and take your bikes along for sightseeing.

and Champlain valleys, near the canal trails we will explore. Later, several key battles of the War of 1812 were fought along these crucial waterways. American troops, hoping to add to the Union, traveled north by water to invade Canada.

Despite this long, bloody history, when peace arrived in 1815 and the borders were finally set, it took only two years until groundbreaking for the Erie Canal and seven years until its completion and opening in 1825. Thus began an era of water-borne commerce which helped shape not only the Empire State but also the nation — an era that continues today.

There are several Erie Canals for you to learn about and explore. First, there is the original Clinton's Ditch of 1825, next an improved Erie Canal, and lastly the functioning Erie Barge Canal. You'll see many historic remnants of the old canal system while watching recreational boats ply the waters of the current waterway.

There's much more to the story. Both the Erie and Champlain canals had many historic "feeders," smaller arteries that connected the main canal to nearby communities and also brought water to the high sections of the main canals. You'll find them all in the pages ahead.

The canals follow the natural waterways which were used by the original inhabitants of the area, the great Iroquois Confederation (or Haudenosaunee). The canal story itself starts with early attempts by some powerful early settlers, the Herkimers and Schuylers, to finance and build privately-owned waterways in the late 1700s. You can still find these old canals in places and you'll learn where in this book. The book doesn't simply tell you to "turn here or there,"

A t the beginning of the 20th century, the state decided to enlarge the Erie Canal and its key feeders once again. This time it was decided to move all the canals, where possible, into adjacent rivers. The Erie was moved into the Mohawk, Oneida, Seneca and Clyde rivers; the Champlain was moved into the Hudson River; the Oswego Canal utilized the Oswego River. Where the use of natural watercourses was not an option, the canals were carried in land-locked sections as before, but much enlarged. Giant locks, 300 feet by 45 feet were now the standard. Depths were 12-15 feet.

The highest single lift-lock in the world was built at Little Falls. No longer were animals used to tow the barges; instead tugboats were the norm. The canals you see today were all completed about 1914. In many respects, they reflect the design and engineering of the Panama Canal, which was being built at the same time, using similar designs. The canals are living history of technology that is just about a century old. But you won't see much freight traffic any longer. Today the canals operate for recreational boaters only. This is becoming one of the great "parks" in the world and each year the cycling gets better.

The small parks at canal locks are good places to start your ride.

it tells you what happened here and there and how to uncover hidden canal history as you ride by. Included are dozens of canal facts that explain the story as you pass by.

Whether you plan to go end-to-end or just explore on a Saturday, this book is designed to help you navigate through the history of the region and to show you how to do it in a way that fits into your schedule. Nearly all canal locks have parks which are good stopping/starting places. You should plan to ride at a leisurely pace since you'll encounter many markers, trail information kiosks, and historic sites. If you like riding trails, since some of the trail surfaces are unpaved you should consider a hybrid or a touring bike with wide tires. For following Bike "5" or Bike "9," standard road tires are best. And since things are changing all the time, I've included a long list of web sites and other resources to help you obtain the most current information.

Our ancestors have left us a great bicycle touring opportunity. Pedaling the routes along New York's canals combines safe and scenic rides, both on-road and along the canal towpaths, with incredible opportunity for insight into early American history. In the chapters ahead, you will find a tour of the canals from one end of New York to the other. The routes are in geographic order from east-to-west and south-to-north, since that's the best way to tie all this great history together logically. You can ride it west-to-east, north-to-south just as easily. All along the way are suggested side-trips and detours. Each year, more and more options are available as new canalway segments are opened. Every stretch you ride will unfold more and more of New York's fascinating canal history. Let's roll!

N ew York State's on-road designated bike routes are the keys to cycling along the canals of New York. They link up all the off-road Canalway Trail segments and they trace other sections of canal where no off-road trails exist. The key two are bike routes "5" and "9." Bike "5" stretches east-to-west, from the Hudson River to Lake Erie, directly along the Erie Canal. Bike "9" stretches south-to-north, from New York City to Montreal. Between Albany and Lake Champlain, it is your indispensable guide to the Champlain Canal. Bike "17" stretches across New York's "Southern Tier" and links up the southern tips of several canals. More numbered on-road bike routes are being implemented; as they are completed, they will help guide you to other canals such as the Genesee Valley Canal. Excellent free maps of Bike Routes "5," "9," and "17" are available. The Resource Guide will advise you how to obtain them.

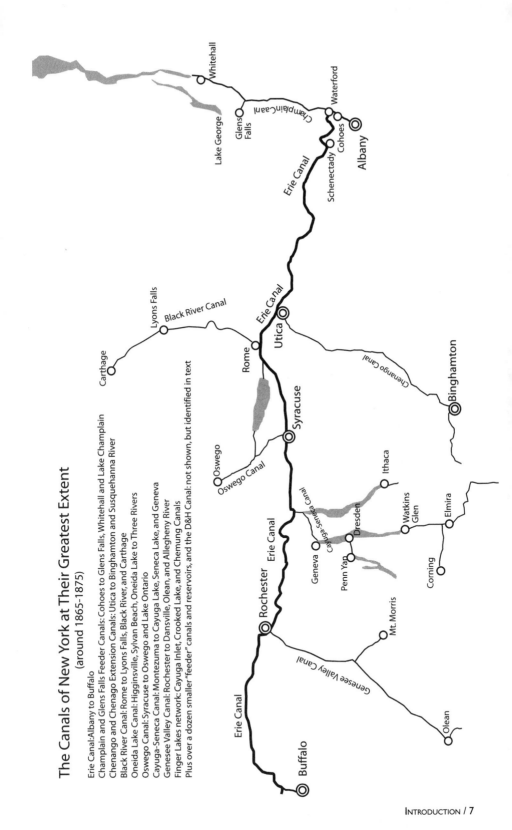

The Canals of New York at Their Greatest Extent
(around 1865-1875)

Erie Canal: Albany to Buffalo
Champlain and Glens Falls Feeder Canals: Cohoes to Glens Falls, Whitehall and Lake Champlain
Chenango and Chenago Extension Canals: Utica to Binghamton and Susquehanna River
Black River Canal: Rome to Lyons Falls, Black River, and Carthage
Oneida Lake Canal: Higginsville, Sylvan Beach, Oneida Lake to Three Rivers
Oswego Canal: Syracuse to Oswego and Lake Ontario
Cayuga-Seneca Canal: Montezuma to Cayuga Lake, Seneca Lake, and Geneva
Genesee Valley Canal: Rochester to Dansville, Olean, and Allegheny River
Finger Lakes network: Cayuga Inlet, Crooked Lake, and Chemung Canals
Plus over a dozen smaller "feeder" canals and reservoirs, and the D&H Canal: not shown, but identified in text

The Bike Routes of Upstate New York

Bike "5" closely follows the route of the Erie Canal. It is about 360 miles long.

Bike "9" traverses the Hudson and Champlain valleys of New York. Starting in New York City, it is approximately 345 miles long.

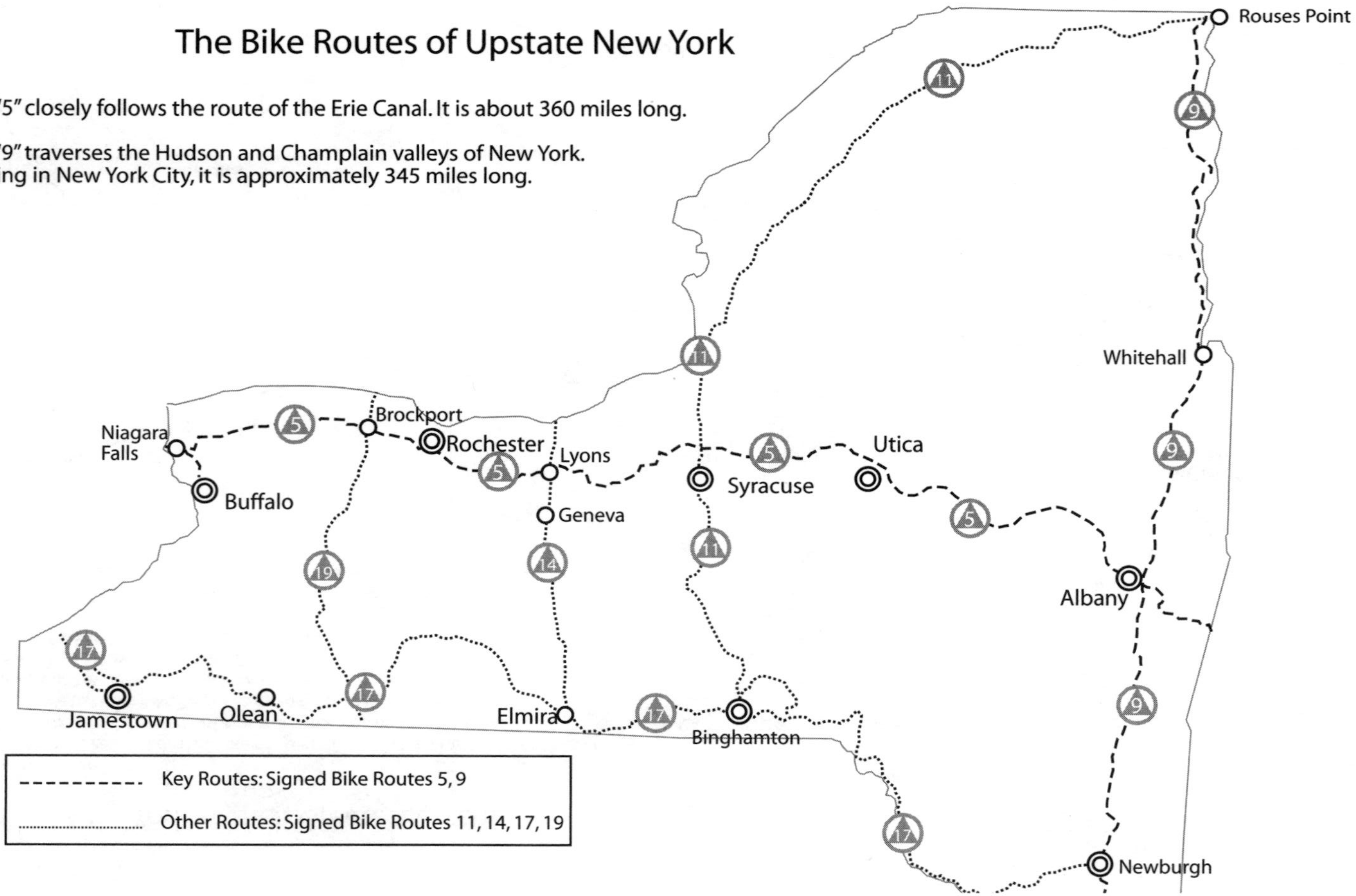

Rouses Point

Whitehall

Newburgh

Albany

Utica

Syracuse

Binghamton

Lyons

Geneva

Elmira

Rochester

Brockport

Olean

Buffalo

Jamestown

Niagara Falls

Key Routes: Signed Bike Routes 5, 9

Other Routes: Signed Bike Routes 11, 14, 17, 19

The Canals
Along the Hudson

*Some of the richest canal history in the United States lies in
New York's capital region and north along the Champlain Canal.
This area offers some wonderful cycling opportunities,
but the sheer number of historic sites, related visitor venues,
and operating canals make touring the canal history of the area
quite complex. Here are several routes to guide you through
this history-filled area.*

Here you can bike to the highest flight of lift-locks in the world, ride
along a flight of five Erie Barge Canal locks near Waterford, and
search out dozens of old hand-crafted stone locks of the earlier Erie and
Champlain Canal alignments in Cohoes. You can visit Phillip Schuyler's
historic home in Albany, his summer residence along the Champlain Canal
in Schuylerville, and learn about his important role in canal building and
many other aspects of American history.

Civil engineers of the 19th century were not yet able to control rivers as
large as the Hudson or Mohawk so they built the original Erie and Champlain
canals and all the other canals entirely apart from major rivers. Both the Erie
and Champlain canals diverged from the Hudson River in Albany, paralleling
it for about seven miles to Cohoes. Here, the Erie and Champlain canals
separated paths with the Champlain heading north through Cohoes, crossing
the Mohawk near today's NY 32 bridge and heading directly north. From
Green Island northward, the Champlain followed the Hudson on its western
shore to Schuylerville, then on its eastern shore to Fort Edward.

The falls at Cohoes are a stunning sight in the spring.

The Erie Canal turned westward in Cohoes and began to climb the Cohoes Falls. Near Crescent, at the NY 9 crossing of the Mohawk River, the Erie, too, also crossed over the Mohawk to its north embankment. At Rexford alongside NY 146 (also known as Aqueduct) the Erie crossed back to the south shore of the Mohawk River. It continued on the south shore through Schenectady and westward. These were the two largest aqueducts on the Erie Canal.

In the 20th century, the Champlain "Barge" Canal was moved into the Hudson River between Waterford and Fort Edward and then the original canal bed was enlarged and followed from Fort Edward to Whitehall. Eleven locks numbered 1-12 (there is no number 10) stretch from Waterford to Whitehall. Connecting to the Champlain Canal at Fort Edward was the Glens Falls Feeder Canal, begun in 1823 and opened in 1828. Today, this opens up a great trail cycling opportunity on the Warren County Bikeway.

With all this canal construction, reconstruction and realignment, the capital region is the most complex part of the whole canal network. The Champlain Canal area is more straight forward, but a great cycling opportunity. So whether you're planning a day trip from Albany up to Waterford or an adventure north to Lake George and perhaps Canada, let's get going.

The original Clinton's Ditch (1817-1825) was not built "in" the great rivers and lakes of New York — the very rivers and lakes that had for centuries shaped and unified the Haudenosaunee, or Five Nations Iroquois Confederacy. Instead, it was built right alongside and entirely separate from the natural waterways.

The locks, gates, weirs and aqueducts were built out of beautifully cut limestone. You can still find and enjoy much of this stonework. The Ditch was only four feet deep. A standard canal lock was ninety feet long, fifteen feet wide, four feet deep, and built of stone. Locks were numbered, starting near its center in Rome, toward the east and west.

Chapter 1

The Capital District

*The cross-state Canalway Trail starts at an attractive waterfront
park right at the Hudson River waterfront adjacent to downtown
Albany. Here, at the junction of Bike "5," Bike "9," and the
Canalway Trail, you are already immersed in history.
This is where Henry Hudson ended his voyage of exploration
for the "Northwest Passage" almost 400 years ago, when
the river became too shallow for his ship, the* Half Moon, *to
proceed. However, if you look up on top of the state university
administration headquarters (former headquarters of the D&H
Railroad), the weathervane is a giant replica of the* Half Moon.
Where Henry Hudson ended his exploration, ours begins.

Y ou can pick up the trail (called the Corning Trail) at the north end of
the parking area. It is a good place to leave your car for a day trip.
If you are looking for secure long-term parking, use one of the nearby private
garages. The Albany County Visitor's Bureau is located along Bike "9" at
Quackenbush Square, very close to your starting point. Contact them for
tourist information, maps, and parking information.

To get to the parking area at the start of the Corning Trail, cross under
I-787. There are two places to do so. You can cross under just on the south
side of the old Delaware & Hudson Railroad Building or further south, at
another underpass under I-787. In either case, once under I-787, follow the
service road northwards. You'll come to a small parking lot which virtually sits
atop the original Erie Canal bed. Remember, if you are parking overnight, it
is best to park in one of the commercial lots in downtown Albany and bike
to the start of the Corning Trail either by riding under I-287 at one of the two
underpasses or by biking over I-787 on the new pedestrian overpass directly
behind the D&H Building.

The Corning Trail at Albany sits on the original basin where the Erie Canal entered the Hudson River just north of this railroad bridge. Today it is a pleasant park – and a great starting point. Just beyond the railroad bridge lies Erie Canal Lock #1, still buried.

If you were going west to Schenectady in the early 1800s, you had two choices: canal boat (taking a full day to navigate the twenty-two locks between Albany and Schenectady) or one of two turnpikes (the Albany and Schenectady, chartered in 1797, and the Great Western, chartered in 1799). After 1831, you might take the Mohawk & Hudson Railroad, the first railroad chartered in America. Today, by bike, you can actually get around faster and see more.

Visiting Albany

Henry Hudson was the only one of the European explorers to sail through the only glacial gap in the Appalachian Mountain chain (near West Point) and beyond for more than 100 miles. There, for his Dutch employers, he found a trading point well inside the Appalachian barrier. It would prove to be very valuable and profitable.

Settled by the Dutch and named Berverwyck ("Beavertown"), Albany is the second oldest state capital in the United States. Only Santa Fe, settled by the Spanish, is older. Albany was not the first capital of New York — that was Nieuw Amsterdam, in the Dutch Colony of Nieuw Netherland. In 1664, the English seized Nieuw Netherland and renamed it New York. Nieuw Amsterdam was renamed New York City and remained the colony's capital. Albany was the new name then given to Berverwyck.

There is a resurgence of interest in the Dutch heritage in New York. The replica of Henry Hudson's ship, "Half Moon", is regularly docked at the Albany waterfront. If it should be there when you bicycle by, be sure to stop and board the ship. The full-size replica, built from historic Dutch documents, is eighty-five feet long.

During the Revolutionary War, the British occupied New York City and as George Washington fled south, the colonial government fled north and ultimately found safety in Albany, where it stayed, making Albany the new capital.

You can make a bicycle tour of Albany, especially on weekends when urban traffic is light. Worth a visit are three homes where major events in the Revolutionary War and the founding of the American republic were played-out: the Schuyler Mansion (1762), the Ten Broeck Mansion (1798), and Cherry Hill (1763). George Washington, Benjamin Franklin, Benedict Arnold, the Marquis de Lafayette and British General Burgoyne were all visitors of the Schuylers. Alexander Hamilton was married at the Schuyler Mansion. (You'll learn further on in this book that Philip Schuyler was one of New York's first canal pioneers, long before DeWitt Clinton.) You can also visit the New York State Museum at the Empire State Plaza, which is expanding its Ice Age exhibits. As you'll discover, the recent Ice Age was the

Louis Rossi

Riverfront Park. D&H Building with weathervane in background.

key to making New York's canals possible. An ice-age mastodont (yes, with a "t"), uncovered near the Cohoes Falls in 1866, is an important part of the exhibit. Finally, the Albany Institute of History and Art is an excellent museum of local history, especially the Dutch period, and has an excellent collection of artifacts from the New York Central Railroad.

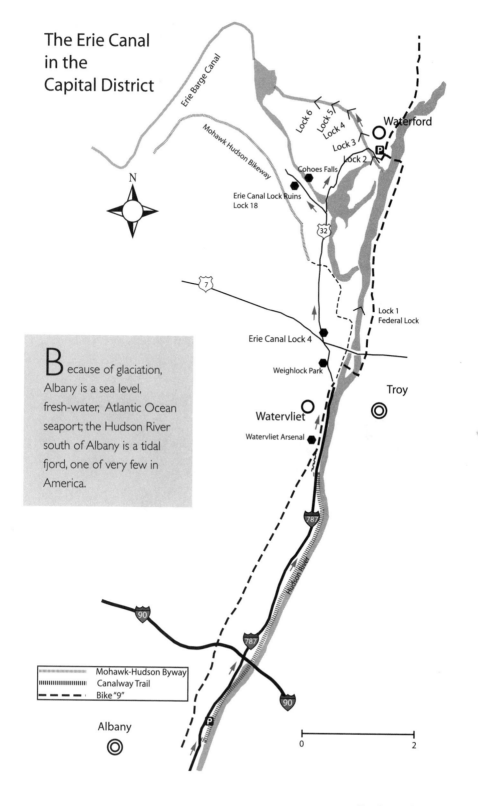

The Erie Canal in the Capital District

Erie Barge Canal

Mohawk Hudson Bikeway

N

Lock 6
Lock 5
Lock 4
Lock 3
Lock 2

Waterford

P

Cohoes Falls

Erie Canal Lock Ruins
Lock 18

32

7

Lock 1
Federal Lock

Erie Canal Lock 4

Weighlock Park

Troy

Watervliet

Watervliet Arsenal

Because of glaciation, Albany is a sea level, fresh-water, Atlantic Ocean seaport; the Hudson River south of Albany is a tidal fjord, one of very few in America.

787

Hudson River

90

787

Mohawk-Hudson Byway
Canalway Trail
Bike "9"

90

Albany

0   2

Albany To Cohoes

Before you start out at the Hudson River waterfront, you will immediately face two options: Bike "9" which is an on-street route following Broadway (NY 32), or the first segment of the Canalway Trail (Corning Trail). Both closely follow the course of the original Erie and the Champlain canals which once headed north from Albany, in one canal bed, directly toward Cohoes. I suggest that you take the Canalway Trail alongside the Hudson River.

The Corning Trail is a pleasant ride directly alongside the Hudson River. It starts almost exactly where Lock 1 of the enlarged Erie Canal lies buried. (The first historic Erie Lock you will actually be able to see is Lock 4, up ahead.) The Erie Canal went north to Watervliet more or less between what is now I-787 and NY 9 (Broadway/Bike "9") and little of it can be seen in these first few miles today. The Corning Trail ends in a small park in Watervliet. You must bike on-road for a few miles from this point. There's a good map of alternative bike routes in the small park where the trail ends. Take a careful look because there are many riding alternatives up ahead. However, the route I recommend, which most closely follows the canal beds, *is not shown* on the map displayed at the park.

Louis Rossi

The start of the Corning Trail.

There is a bit of bike path history here. The name "Corning Trail" seems to be disappearing from this short pathway. In a way, that is sad. The trail is named for Albany Mayor Erastus Corning III, who was mayor for almost fifty years. Thirty years ago, the Hudson River waterfront at Albany was a wasteland. Back then, Governor Rockefeller, Mayor Corning, and Transportation Commissioner Hennessy had the vision to use interstate highway funds, when this was unheard of, to create the urban riverfront parkland and bike path that we see today. This may not seem like much today, but it was a big thing then. Rockefeller, Corning, and Hennessy are forgotten bike champs. If somewhere along an interstate highway elsewhere in America you find yourself cycling along a separate bike path, think of Albany and these visionaries. Interestingly, Mayor Corning was a great grandson of the original Erastus Corning who devised the idea of unifying the dozen or so small railroads that stretched across New York State into the New York Central Railroad, which would become one of the greatest transportation companies in America under the direction of the Vanderbilt family. The Corning family pioneered both rail and bike transportation development.

Go under I-787 and take an immediate right onto Broadway in Watervliet. In a few short blocks, Bike "9" joins from the left. Up ahead, you might want to stop and visit the Watervliet Arsenal. The Arsenal, founded in 1813, remains the last American manufacturer of cannon. Once employing ten thousand, the Arsenal now has less than five hundred workers. The museum, spanning almost two hundred years, contains many historic and interesting buildings and a detailed history of the manufacture of cannon. It is well worth a visit either this trip or later on — you will be cycling right by the main gate on Broadway. You must pass through security, but visitors are welcome.

Just past the arsenal, NY 32 turns left while Bike "9" and the Mohawk-Hudson Bike-Hike Trail continue straight. In order to closely follow the canal, turn left, leave Bike "9" and follow NY 32. NY 32 immediately turns again (right) toward the north. Now you are directly adjacent to the original canals, which are on your immediate right. In a few blocks is the first important canal historic site. At Second Avenue (NY 32) and Twenty-fifth Street in Colonie (just north of the Watervliet City line) is a small park identifying the site of the eastern Weighlock building which once stood here. (When you get to Onondaga County you can see an actual weighlock.) This is a pleasant space to stop and see the lock foundations and read the historic markers.

Just above this point, the improved Erie Canal of the 1840s separated from the original alignment and began its climb over the Cohoes Falls. To see the first of these impressive cobblestone locks, just a few blocks further on, turn left off Broadway (NY 32) onto Elm Street and you'll come to a newly restored Erie Canal Lock #4. This is the first of the Erie Canal locks you can actually see (Locks 1, 2 and 3 are there but not yet uncovered), and the first of

Early canal builders faced formidable obstacles at the junction of the Mohawk and Hudson rivers. To go west, the Erie Canal would first have to overcome 169-foot fall of the Mohawk River at Cohoes. To head north, the Champlain Canal had to cross the delta of a complex series of channels and islands stretching over two miles where the powerful Mohawk River enters the Hudson River.

fourteen locks needed to overcome the height of the Cohoes Falls. This short quarter-mile detour is worthwhile. After seeing Lock 4, return to NY 32 and continue north toward Cohoes.

As you head into Cohoes on Broadway, the old Champlain Canal will be on your right. You'll come to a historical marker identifying "Juncta," which is where Clinton's Ditch and the Champlain Canal parted in 1825. There is not much there now but about two hundred years ago, "Juncta" was one of the most important and bustling centers of commerce in North America.

Wildly successful beyond its builder's imaginations, the Erie Canal was immediately overwhelmed with traffic. Right away and continually for the rest of the 19th century, the canal was enlarged and improved. It was deepened; double locks were built and then enlarged again. Ever greater aqueducts were built. Locks were now 100 feet long, 18 feet wide and 7 feet (later 9) deep. Now, all locks were numbered from Albany. As before, all of this was still kept separate from the natural rivers, which were still too large to be controlled by engineering of that time. And again, after every widening and improvement, still more traffic crowded the waterway. When you visit old Erie Canal sites, most of what you now see is the construction from this period.

Lock 18 is near Cohoes Falls.

Visiting Canal Sites in Cohoes

The best way to understand the complex canal history unfolding before you is to go the Cohoes Visitors Center in downtown Cohoes, located on Remsen Street two blocks west of NY 32. This is an outstanding museum of local history. You'll learn that Cohoes was once the "Knitting Capital of the World." Pick up a self-guided tour brochure that is indispensable if you want to trace the enormous canal history in Cohoes.

Discovering old lock sites in Cohoes is not easy since there are so many. Remember that the Erie and Champlain canals separated from each other here. There are three old canal alignments in Cohoes: two Erie Canal alignments (the original Clinton's Ditch of 1825 and the improved Erie Canal of 1840s), and the Champlain Canal. Let's explore.

Lock 18, a National Register of Historic Places site, is the best-preserved lock. It is easy to find being near the Cohoes Falls, just off Mohawk Street, before the turn up Manor Street to the Mohawk-Hudson Bikepath. Lock 18 brought the Erie Canal to an elevation of 188 feet above sea level. This was high enough to enable the canal to be carried over the Mohawk River on a stone aqueduct up ahead at Crescent.

Be sure not to miss the overlook that faces Cohoes Falls. There is a small park on your right at the top of the Mohawk Street climb, off Cataract Street. These falls were a sacred place to the Mohawk Indians. Indian lore explains that the Mohawk Indian Hiawatha conceived of the Iroquois Confederation while meditating at this spot. Since the Mohawk is the source of water for today's canal locks, the falls can only be seen in full splendor during the spring. In the autumn after a dry summer, all the water is diverted for canal usage, leaving the falls dry.

Locks 9-12 and 14-17 are also visible. Including Lock 18, that's nine Erie locks in only two miles. If you want to explore, you'll find the old Erie Canal right-of-way hidden along Devlin Street and Summit Street in the west end of Cohoes, and then along Olmstead, Sargeant, and between Central and Lincoln on the south end. Some of it is attractive, some is industrial, and some is downright unsightly. However, there are two small parks, Alexander Street Park and George Street Park, which are not too difficult to find and contain Erie Canal lock ruins.

Erie Canal Lock 9 is typical of the many historic structures in Cohoes.

As there are two old Erie Canal alignments in Cohoes, all this can be a bit confusing. But it is great history. As you will learn if you stop at the visitors center, the original Clinton's Ditch was converted into sluiceways and power canals for the water-powered textile industry which flourished here. Historic signs along North Mohawk Street will help you interpret the story of the first Erie Canal alignment.

The route of the Champlain Canal is easier to locate. The Champlain Canal did not have to climb the Cohoes Falls. It crossed the Mohawk at a height of only 32 feet above sea level, behind a dam in the vicinity of the present NY 32 bridge. As a result, it had fewer locks. Today, the old Champlain Canal alignment can be found between what is currently NY 32 and NY 787. Champlain Canal Lock 2 is visible just a few feet north of the intersection of Spring Street and NY 787, on the west side of NY 787. Lock 4 is on the north side of the Mohawk River in Waterford.

Surely, some of the greatest canal history in the world is within and near Cohoes. Enjoy the challenge of doing your own exploration.

Visiting Waterford Sites

No trip to visit canal sites in the Capital Region should miss the sites in Waterford. Like Cohoes, Waterford is rich in canal lore. From Cohoes, bike north on NY 32 and cross the Mohawk River. Immediately on your right you'll see a small sign indicating a pathway along the Champlain Canal. Take this

Louis Rossi

The old Champlain Canal towpath in the town of Waterford gives a sense of what canals were like over a century ago.

route and you'll find yourself atop an original segment of Champlain Canal towpath at old Champlain Canal Lock 4.

This short stretch of path is unpaved. If you find it very wet, it may be difficult to bike; if so, simply stay on NY 32 which will also take you directly into Waterford. Both the Champlain Canal towpath and NY 32 take you directly to another very important destination — the Waterford Harbor Visitors Center and Erie Barge Canal Lock 2. Be sure to visit both sites, which are adjacent to each other. There is a great deal of historical and interpretive material at both locations. There is safe parking at both places.

Jim Cassatt

The sign welcoming you to Waterford will tell you that it is the oldest incorporated village in America (1794). Waterford is a pleasant historic canal town working to preserve its canal heritage. Dozens of small frame houses and narrow streets give this area a unique architectural character.

Locktenders are great sources of information.

Waterford is the eastern hub of today's canal system as well as an important junction on the historic Champlain Canal, so you should plan to spend some time here. It is a good location for a daytrip. Both the Waterford Harbor Visitors Center and Erie Barge Canal Lock 2 have excellent interpretive information on the old Erie and old Champlain canals (three old Champlain Canal locks are preserved here, adjacent to Erie Barge Canal Lock 2), plus excellent information on the modern Erie. Talk to the locktender and tap into a wealth of information.

While in Waterford, be sure to take the dead-end trip up and down the Flight of Locks Road. This is the highest flight of locks in the world. As you go by Lock 3, look across the canal and you'll see the Waterford canal shops and dry docks. These shops, not open to the public, are a veritable museum of industrial America. Built "new" in 1914, they continue to make the various pieces of unique canal paraphernalia that enable the canals to operate today. In a little over two miles, at the top of the climb, note the twin set of guard gates — these can completely close the canal for protection against damage in the winter and for maintenance. There is a small park and a nice rest stop at the top of the flight.

If you are going to follow the Champlain Canal northbound, all you need to do is go back to the center of Waterford and take 3rd Street, which is Bike "9." You'll be following Bike "9" for some sixty more miles to Whitehall. It's a trip rich in both canal and Revolutionary War history and is described in the next chapter.

If you are going to follow the Erie Canal westward, you need to return to Cohoes (See Chapter 4) and pick up the Canalway Trail.

Robert Donahue

The new Waterford Harbor Visitor's Center is a great bike ride start point.

Chapter 2

The Champlain Canal

During the Revolutionary War, British General Burgoyne designed a three-pronged invasion to divide the colonies. One force would come from Canada in the north, another from New York City, and a third from Lake Ontario in the west. The target was Albany. All three invasions failed. The largest of the British forces, led by Burgoyne down from Canada, eventually surrendered at Saratoga. The army from Lake Ontario withdrew at Fort Stanwix and the one from New York never made it past Kingston. This ride along the Champlain Canal not only parallels Burgoyne's 1777 route, it also passes many Revolutionary War sites. There is so much to see that allowing three or even four days would be wise depending on your cycling abilities and interest in history.

Bike "9," the continuous route from New York City to the Canadian border near Montreal, is the best guide for exploring the Champlain Canal. The segment between Waterford and Whitehall is being developed into a "scenic byway" by Saratoga and Washington counties and you can find some very interesting segments of the old Champlain Canal towpaths in Waterford, Schuylerville, and Fort Edward. The Champlain Barge Canal is open to boating and operational the whole distance. Like the Erie Barge Canal, every lock has a small park so use them for rest stops or as excellent bases for day trips. The villages along the way are well spaced for food and drink stops and for checking out local historical sites.

Travel Tip

Amtrak's "Adirondack" passenger train, with stops all along the Bike "9" Champlain Canal corridor, has special baggage facilities that cater to bicyclists. This expands loop and out-and-back options as well as trips north to Canada.

The Champlain Canal was built to connect the Hudson River, which flows south to the Atlantic, with Lake Champlain, which flows north into the Saint Lawrence River. The history of the Champlain Canal is closely linked with that of the Erie Canal. Both were begun in 1817, soon after peace came to a territory that had known brutal warfare for almost two centuries. Both followed unsuccessful attempts by private companies to construct navigational improvements. The Champlain Canal opened in 1823, two years earlier than the Erie. Somehow, the Champlain never seemed to get respect. Perhaps that was because a canal linking the northern end of Lake Champlain and the Saint Lawrence River, all in Canada, was not completed until 1843. Perhaps it was because of America's fascination with the opening and settlement of the West. In any case, the Champlain, like the Erie, was a vast commercial success. Also like the Erie, and important to us here, is the role the route along the canal plays in linking together much of early American history.

Saratoga County: Waterford to Schuylerville

While today's Champlain Barge Canal starts in Waterford in Saratoga County, the original canal separated from the Erie Canal at "Juncta," in Cohoes in Albany County. So there are a few historical old locks and a short stretch of old towpath open for cycling described in the previous chapter. There are also some important sites to visit in Waterford — all described in the previous chapter.

After you have visited Waterford, you are ready to start north, on Bike "9." From Waterford, it is just about sixty miles to Lake Champlain at Whitehall and this short distance is packed with history.

Back in the early 1800s, the original Champlain Canal was built parallel to but separate from the Hudson River. The initial canal followed the west shore of the river northward from Waterford to Schuylerville. Then, for a few years, it used the river to reach Fort Edward, but that option worked poorly and soon a canal bed was dug along the east shore just north of Schuylerville. As noted earlier, the old towpath is being opened for recreational use. Largely intact, it waits to be re-developed. You will see many signs of the old Champlain Canal alignment as you pedal north.

Bike "9" turns north onto 3rd Street in Waterford. In two miles you will pass a historic marker indicating the furthest north point reached by the crew of Henry Hudson. In the same year that Henry Hudson's crew reached this point, just a few months earlier in 1609, Samuel de Champlain reached what is now Ticonderoga, about seventy-five miles to the north. There, at the instigation of his Huron allies, de Champlain launched a punitive raid against the Iroquois. This began more than a century of hostility between the Iroquois and the French, and a strong permanent alliance between the Iroquois and the Dutch and British.

Lock 2 Canal Park in Waterford contains excellent interpretive material on both the Erie and Champlain canals.

Continue north, passing through Mechanicville to Stillwater, eleven miles from Waterford. There, in Stillwater, you will find a historic blockhouse immediately adjacent to Bike "9." There is also an attractive canal park at Lock 4 in Stillwater. To get there, leave Bike "9" and cross over the bridge over the Hudson and turn immediately to your right. Not too visible, but just beside the Lock 4 canal park, the Hoosic River enters the Hudson River from the east.

From Stillwater, for the next dozen miles, you will be passing through the various historical sites that mark the wide-ranging Battle of Saratoga. Plan to take your time — historic markers abound. There are plenty on both sides of the Hudson, identifying all the sites of the many skirmishes that took place as the British tried to attack and then retreat from the blocking American forces.

The entrance to the Saratoga National Historical Park is on your left on Bike "9." Be sure

The Emita II, a retrofitted 1953 Maine ferryboat now used for canal trips, approaches Lock 4 near Stillwater.

Warren County

Glens Falls

To Whitehall

Hudson Falls

Fort Edward

Lock 7

Champlain Canal
Waterford to Hudson Falls

Washington County

Lock 6

Fort Miller

Saratoga County

To Saratoga Springs

Schuylerville

Lock 5

Saratoga National
Historical Park

Champlain Barge Canal

Stillwater

Lock 4

Lock 3

Mechanicville

Lock 2

| — — — — — — | Bike "9" |

Lock 1

Waterford

6 5 4
3
Cohoes Lock 2

0   5

There is a significant bit of untold canal history here. First, the Hoosic River extends southeastward to the border of New York and Vermont; it crosses the southeast tip of Vermont and enters northeastern Massachusetts where its source is found high in the Berkshire Mountains. For centuries, the powerful Mohawk Indians used this waterway to dominate the Indians of New England. It was the watercourse followed by General Burgoyne's troops to the historic Battle of Walloomsac (Battle of Bennington) during the Revolution. Later, the Commonwealth of Massachusetts considered using the Hoosic as a route for a cross-Massachusetts canal that would link Boston with the Erie Canal. This canal was never built, because a four-mile canal tunnel would have been required to bring the canal under the Berkshires. It was impossible to even try this back in the early 1800s. However, the tunnel was ultimately built as a railroad tunnel (1851-1875) and is still one of the longest railroad tunnels in the world.

to take this detour. There is an entrance fee for cyclists. The park contains a nine-mile paved loop that will take you to all the important sites of the Battle of 1777. Allow yourself several hours as the National Park Service has done a wonderful job of highlighting the principal events of the multi-day battle which took place here. The loop is a quiet one-way roadway that takes you to the commanding heights that the American forces occupied to halt the British advance. The interpretive center will give you much information about the many battles that comprised this campaign, which extended into Hubbardton (near Rutland, Vermont) and Walloomsac (near Bennington, Vermont). This was no small campaign. It included naval engagements on Lake Champlain. Thousands of troops of many nationalities were assembled and competently commanded in what was certainly a vast wilderness.

Had General Burgoyne succeeded in reaching Albany, and the British campaign in the Mohawk Valley been successful, the colonies would have been split in two. Instead, the defeat at Saratoga, coupled

You will pass dozens of historic markers and sites in this history-packed area.

One of America's most competent commanders in this complex battle, and the founder of the American navy at Whitehall (which comes near the end of this tour), was Benedict Arnold. There is a memorial to him at the battlefield, but, as he had subsequently deserted and gone to the British side, and Benedict Arnold had become synonymous with traitor, his name was omitted. You'll see this on the park loop road. At the 155-foot obelisk commemorating the Battle at Schuylerville, there are spaces for four enormous statues. The one blank wall is for Arnold.

with the losses in the Mohawk Valley at Oriskany and Fort Stanwix were the first major American victories. The prospect of defeating the British brought the essential Dutch and French support that was necessary for the Revolution to succeed.

When you exit the battlefield, return to Bike "9" and continue north. At Schuylerville, the Phillip Schuyler House (1777) where General Burgoyne surrendered is roadside. Also near Schuylerville is the 155-foot tall Saratoga Battlefield Monument, a short climb to the west. Road signs will help you locate it easily. The monument, built between 1877 and 1883, has been thoroughly reconditioned by the National Park Service. You can climb to an overlook at the top of the obelisk.

Tom Eagan

A historic overlook at the Saratoga Battlefield. American forces and cannons posted here closed off the Hudson Valley route to Albany.

A new Canal Visitors Center has been opened in Schuylerville; it is an excellent stop for the latest local tourist information. It is located directly off Bike Route "9" on the old Champlain Canal towpath. Adjacent to the visitors center is a newly opened stretch of Champlain Canal towpath. This towpath (unpaved, but in very good condition) connects the Schuyler House on the south with a small park at Champlain Barge Canal Lock 5. This canal park contains ruins of old Champlain Canal Lock 9.

Follow Bike "9" north from Schuylerville. Just outside the village, look for the canal park at Barge Canal Lock 5. There is an old Champlain Canal Lock at this small park. This was the site of the only major Champlain Canal aqueduct, which carried the original canal over and across the Hudson River. Boat tours are available there.

A Note on Visiting Schuylerville

This is a pretty small village where many critically important things happened. Plan to spend some time. First, this was the home of the Schuylers. The Schuylers were the original Dutch patroons for this area. The Dutch method of settlement, unique in New York of all the colonies, was to grant vast tracts of land to "patroons" who would then develop their properties. One of the positives of this approach was the Schuylers' deep interest in development of their lands. Perhaps, Philip Schuyler was the real father of New York's canals. He was the force behind the two private companies (Northern Inland Navigation Company and Western Inland Navigation Company), which built privately-financed locks and dams at critical sites along the Erie and Champlain canals in the late 1700s. This was after he had successfully fought off the British Army under General Burgoyne, after he wed his daughter to Alexander Hamilton, and accomplished a number of other achievements any one of which would be enough to satisfy a contemporary American. Be sure to visit the Schuyler homes in Schuylerville and Albany to get the full story.

Washington County: Schuylerville to Fort Edward

Continuing north, follow Bike "9," NY 4, across the Hudson River and enter Washington County. It is a pleasant and scenic ten-mile trip northward along the Hudson to Fort Edward. Along the way you will find many historic markers dealing with the Champlain Canal, the French and Indian War, and the Revolutionary War.

About a mile into Washington County, you'll see a sign for the old Champlain Canal Lock 12 on your right. A mile further, at the entrance to Champlain Barge Canal Lock 6, there's a stone marker identifying the route General Knox used to bring Fort Ticonderoga's cannon to George Washington at Boston. General Knox brought the cannon down frozen Lake George, then overland through Fort Edward and down along the Hudson to Albany. He then hauled them eastward into Massachusetts. Then take the small road (River Road) which passes directly in front of Lock 6. It will take you close to the Hudson River, past the site of Fort Miller (1693), and return you to Bike "9" further north.

Many bridges across the canal, like the road to Fort Miller at Lock 6, have steel decks. Be careful riding across them, especially if they are wet.

Along Bike "9," you will pass the site of Jane McCrae's July 27, 1777 slaughter (she was later reburied in Fort Edward). The murder of Jane McCrea, by Indians in General Burgoyne's army, was an important milestone in the Revolutionary War. Daughter of a loyalist, she was being escorted to the British lines by Indian allies when she was killed by them. This action galvanized anti-British sentiment throughout the colonies and brought thousands of militia into the war. If British-allied Indians were going to kill loyalist civilians, what would they do to revolutionary families? Remember, too, the massacre of the British troops and civilians evacuating Fort William Henry in the French and Indian wars was not too distant in time or place.

You'll pass Barge Canal Lock 7 as you enter Fort Edward. You'll immediately encounter a number of historic sites. Excavations are underway at the site of the encampment of Roger's Rangers; this was the launching point for one of America's major invasions of Canada. Over fifteen thousand soldiers once camped at this site over two hundred and fifty years ago. Visit the Old Fort House (1772), which is immediately on your left as you enter town. The museum is really a complex of five buildings and contains an exhibit on Jane McCrea. Almost opposite the museum, across Bike "9," is an old Glens Falls Feeder aqueduct.

At Fort Edward, the Hudson River turns westward. Here, you have options. I'll describe the ride to Whitehall first, as this is the route of the Champlain Canal. In the next chapter, I'll describe a detour along the historic and well-maintained Glens Falls Feeder Canal. In 1777, General Burgoyne used both routes simultaneously to move his Army southward. If you can

Aqueduct ruins at Fort Edward.

only do one, I recommend that you go along the Glens Falls Feeder Canal to Glens Falls and the Warren County Bikeway to Lake George. Better still, base yourself in the area and ride both routes on different days.

Washington County: Fort Edward to Whitehall

Bike "9" is your key to the twenty-four mile stretch of canal between Fort Edward and Whitehall. The old Champlain Canal and the present barge canal followed the same route. As you speed by, think of General Burgoyne's troops. They moved southward in this area at barely one mile per day because a thousand American troops, under General Schuyler, moved ahead of them felling trees, flooding trails, and otherwise imposing obstacles to their forward progress.

Bike "9" follows NY 4. This is an excellent, fast cycling route through rolling hills and farms. The road from Fort Ann to Whitehall is a busy, but there are excellent shoulders. There are some quieter local roads to follow and explore, which you can find with a good Washington County road map, but use Bike "9" as your primary guide.

The site of Fort Edward.

*Whitehall, the birthplace of the U.S. Navy, is at the northern end of the
Champlain Canal.*

You'll pass the summit section of the Champlain Barge Canal, which
extends for six miles between Locks 8 and 9. (There is no Lock 10.) The
Glens Falls Feeder Canal (next chapter) helps keep this summit full of water.
Throughout this portion of your trip, the modern Champlain Canal sits on top
of the original canal alignment. The Champlain Canal summit is about 120 feet
above sea level. A rise of just 120 feet is all that separates the Atlantic waters
from those that flow into the Saint Lawrence. With mountains towering over
4000 feet in all directions, it took the last Ice Age, and the glacial scouring of
the Polar Ice Cap to carve this flat, almost sea-level passageway.

You can stop at Lock 11, between Fort Ann and Whitehall, for a rest.
When you reach Whitehall, continue on Bike "9" until you see a sign for "Lock
12 Marina." Turn here. It will take you to the center of town, alongside the
canal and to the museum sites. Lock 12, which replaces three old locks that
stood at this site, marks the end of the Champlain Canal. Here the canal enters
Lake Champlain, which extends the reach of the canal more than one hundred
miles north into Canada.

Whitehall is the true birthplace of the American navy. This picturesque community, originally named Skenesborough, is considered the birthplace of the U.S. Navy since the first fleet of ships was built here in 1776 during the American Revolution. The Whitehall Urban Cultural Park Visitors Center/ Skenesborough Museum is packed with historical information and ship models from the Revolution and War of 1812.

It is thirty-five miles across Washington County from the Hudson River, above Schuylerville, to Whitehall, on Bike "9." The various side trips described above will lengthen your ride.

This is the northern end of the Champlain Canal. Are you heading back to Albany? If so, retrace your steps. Are you going north to the Adirondacks and Canada? If so, Bike "9" remains your guide. At the end of the next chapter, you'll find some useful information on the historic sites that lie just ahead and the best routes to use heading north along Lake Champlain toward Canada.

In Whitehall, in 1775, Benedict Arnold commissioned the first ship and the first fleet which would become the U.S. Navy. With a fleet of seventeen small ships, fourteen of which were built at Whitehall, Arnold sailed north to engage a British fleet near Plattsburgh in 1776. Although most of Arnold's fleet was ultimately captured or destroyed by the British in a three-day battle, its very existence had delayed invasion plans. This important engagement in the British campaign to descend the Champlain Valley to Albany was ultimately resolved at Saratoga. Here you can see historic naval artifacts, including the hull of the USS Niagara from the War of 1812. Be sure to stop at the excellent Whitehall Visitors Center at the Skenesborough Museum adjacent to the canal, just one block east of Bike "9." There is a lot of history here, and the local guides can give you the most up-to-date information.

Chapter 3

The Glens Falls Feeder Canal and Warren County Bikeway

The Glens Falls Feeder Canal Trail and the Warren County Bikeway are two scenic rides that can be hooked together for a great day round-trip of about thirty miles. Both routes are packed with history and feature scenic off-road riding. We will also explore a trip northward to Canada.

Glens Falls Feeder Canal

The Glens Falls Feeder Canal extended navigation to Glens Falls by bringing water from the Upper Hudson River to feed the summit level of the Champlain Canal. The Glens Falls Feeder Canal Trail is on the old towpath and is unpaved but well maintained. It is seven miles of great scenic and historic bicycling.

The ride begins on Bike "9" in Fort Edward. Follow Bike "9" uphill until you cross over the railroad and pass Fort Edward High School. Turn right on County Route 37 (Burgoyne Road) and ride two miles until you come to signs identifying the Glens Falls Feeder Canal Heritage Trail. You'll intersect the trail at a small park. On your immediate right is a remarkable canal site, a flight of five original "Combine Locks." These are very interesting and impressive because the five locks were never enlarged and are in their original fifteen-foot width. This is perhaps the best place in New York State where you can see what a flight of locks of the original Clinton's Ditch looked like.

After visiting the Combine Locks, turn around and take the trail westward toward Glens Falls. The trail follows the towpath of this historic, virtually "original" segment of canal. Along the way, you'll find excellent interpretive

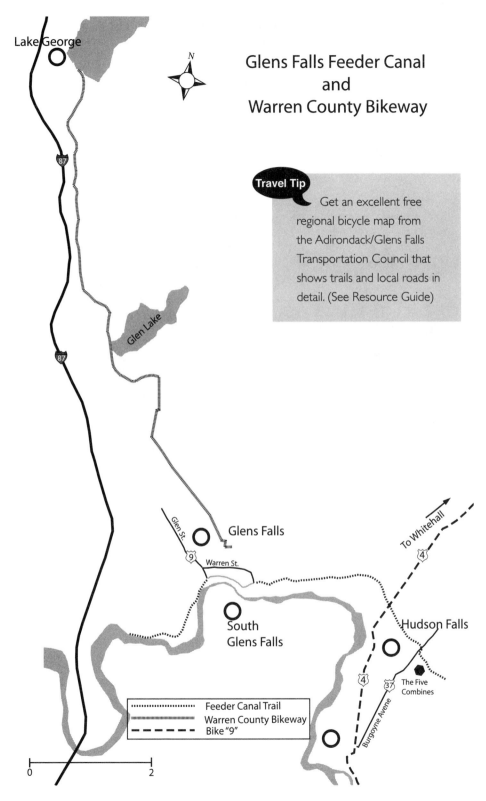

Lake George

Glen Lake

**Glens Falls Feeder Canal
and
Warren County Bikeway**

Travel Tip Get an excellent free regional bicycle map from the Adirondack/Glens Falls Transportation Council that shows trails and local roads in detail. (See Resource Guide)

Glen St.

Glens Falls

Warren St.

South
Glens Falls

To Whitehall

Hudson Falls

The Five
Combines

Burgoyne Avene

.... Feeder Canal Trail
|||||||||||||||| Warren County Bikeway
– – – Bike "9"

0   2

The Five Combine Locks. In canal days, it took fifteen minutes to traverse each lock, dropping eleven feet with each step.

signs explaining the history of this small canal. Don't go so fast that you miss the "Turn Around Basin" at Martindale Street. The basin was once large enough to hold sixty canal boats; today it is a small park. Further along, the path switches to the other canal bank.

As the trail enters Glens Falls, there is a short discontinuity. The path ends at Shermantown Road so take Warren Street westward. You'll pass the Hyde Collection, an art museum and historic house featuring an impressive and eclectic collection of art (Botticelli, da Vinci, Rembrandt, Picasso, Whistler, Modigliani, to name but a few.) Further along Warren Street, you'll come to Glen Street (NY 9).

Continue on the two-mile dead end stretch of the feeder canal trail that extends westward from Glen Street. This is an attractive stretch with additional interpretive signs. You can now check out Glens Falls, an attractive small city in the foothills of the Adirondacks, retrace your route down the feeder canal trail, or head north toward Lake George.

Warren County Bikeway

The Warren County Bikeway has good trail signage linking it and the feeder canal trail. It starts three blocks north of Warren Street, just north of the Hyde Collection, and runs all the way to Lake George. This route is approximately ten miles of excellent paved bikeway. There are two short, clearly marked, safe and easy to follow on-road segments.

The bikeway is built on an old Delaware & Hudson Railway branch line that follows the route described in detail in *The Last of the Mohicans* as "the rude path." Some of the trail was once an old military road from Fort William Henry to Fort Edward and was later used by General Knox in the famous trek to haul fifty-nine cannons to Boston during the winter of 1775/1776.

Those who read *The Last of the Mohicans*, or saw the movie, may recall the cave, beneath a waterfall, where Hawkeye, Cora, Alice, Uncas, Chingachcook, and Major Heyward took refuge. That cave actually exists. It lies beneath the waterfall at Glens Falls. To see it, you'll need to go south halfway across the NY 9 Bridge. You can see the cave from the walkway. The bridge will take you over the falls that Cooper employed in his narrative; the cave is now beneath the bridge and the site is marked.

This bike path is one of the most distinctive, attractive, and historic in all New York. At certain points, it enters dense Adirondack woods that seem as forbidding today as they must have seemed to Cooper's characters. One can easily imagine skillful Indian warriors ambushing redcoats. You'll find that this is

Louis Rossi

The Warren County Bikeway is an excellent paved route from Glens Falls to Lake George.

quite hilly for a rail trail. As you climb, think of the laboring steam locomotives hauling passenger trains laden with tourists along this route.

You'll enjoy a long downhill coast to the Village of Lake George. The trail ends near Lake George Beach State Park where there are many historic markers. The park is filled with erratics, boulders that clearly don't belong to the terrain in which they are found. It's the glaciers again. These boulders were transported here, in the ice, from regions far to the north. Because the historic battlefields around the old fort were never farmed, they lie mostly as the glaciers left them. Lake George once flowed south and into the Hudson River. You are standing on glacial deposits between Lake George Village and Glens Falls, which dammed up the lake and reversed its flow so that it now flows north into Lake Champlain and the Saint Lawrence.

Boulders (erratics) at the Lake George State Park. Note the excursion boat in the background.

Lake George Village, a tourist spot, has a popular beach and a variety of attractions. For those interested in the French and Indian Wars, there are many sights to see. Fort William Henry (1755) is faithfully recreated. The Marquis de Montcalm, heading up a force of ten thousand, attacked and defeated the British defenders of the fort. The fort was destroyed. Contrary to the terms of surrender, Montcalm's Indian allies massacred the British and colonials right along the route of the bikeway. There are a number of historic markers in close proximity to the fort which help interpret the complex warfare which took place here.

Going North to Canada

Lake Champlain hooks up with the Champlain Canal and then, in Canada, with the Chambly Canal, which allows water traffic to get to the Saint Lawrence River. It is 163 scenic miles from Lake George to Montreal. If you plan to continue north, Bike "9" will be your primary guide, but plan to take the boat from Lake George Village. While Bike "9" is a pretty flat route overall, the few short miles north of Whitehall and south of Ticonderoga contain very steep climbs. It is a scenic route, great for the climber. A wiser cyclist will trace the invasion routes used in the French and Indian Wars and take the magnificent thirty-eight mile boat trip across Lake George. Get the early-morning boat in Lake George Village and take it to Baldwin Landing (Fort Ticonderoga). Be sure to make reservations in advance as this boat trip is not daily. Bicyclists are welcome, but they need to know you are coming in advance. The boat trip is well worth the time and money. Whether you arrive in Ticonderoga by boat from Lake George Village or by Bike "9" from Whitehall, be sure to visit Fort Ticonderoga (1755). It was the guns from this fort, captured by Ethan Allen, that were hauled overland to George Washington's forces at Boston. Once he had obtained this weaponry, Washington was able to force the British to withdraw from Boston.

Travel Tip
Excellent bicycle touring information on cycling in Vermont and New York is available from Lake Champlain Bikeways. Once in Quebec, Canada, the best source of bicycling information is Route Verte. They can provide the best information about on-road and off-road bicycle routes. Both websites are listed in the Resource Guide.

From Ticonderoga northward to Montreal, Bike "9" is an excellent rolling route that closely follows Lake Champlain. There is one big climb between Willsboro and Keeseville. Several attractive villages along the lake are perfect for food and lodging.

A visit to the forts at Crown Point (ten miles further north of Ticonderoga on Bike "9") is essential. These are great historic sites with outstanding interpretive information to help grasp the amazing history of this region. This requires a three and one-half mile diversion off Bike "9" to the Crown Point Bridge where the state maintains an interesting historical site featuring several forts.

Just before you enter Plattsburgh, you can see Valcour Island on your right. This was the site of Benedict Arnold's naval battle with the British during the Revolutionary War — where the American Navy began. Plattsburg is a small, attractive city with a number of historic sites. City Hall contains a museum of the naval battles that occurred nearby.

There is still more canal tourism in Canada. The 20-km Chambly Canal towpath (dating from 1843) is almost 100 percent open for off-road cycling. Quebec is very bicycle-friendly and in addition to the canal towpaths, there are many local roads that are great for cycling.

If you consider the reach of the Champlain Canal from Albany all the way to the Saint Lawrence River, you can appreciate the navigational achievement it was when it was put in operation over a century and a half ago. Operational today, it is a treasure of historic sites and a scenic cycling opportunity.

Travel Tip
The Albany-Montreal "Adirondack" is equipped to carry bicycles and makes seven stops along the west shore of Lake Champlain between Whitehall and Rouses Point.

The Canals of
the Mohawk Valley

The cycling along the Mohawk River between Schenectady and Rome is some of the best that New York has to offer—navigation is a lot easier for a cyclist and there are many things to see along the way. This is because the original Erie Canal never left the south shore of the Mohawk River, making its historic sites easier to find.

The original Clinton's Ditch was built entirely outside the Mohawk River along its southern embankment. The 19th century enlargements to the Erie Canal were all either atop or alongside the original "Ditch." This was all abandoned early in the 20th century when the Erie was modernized again and moved into the Mohawk River. While much of the original canal bed is lost, nearly all the original stone aqueducts and locks remain.

"Bike 5," the on-road ride, follows the canal routes closely. Across the valley, large portions of an abandoned railroad, directly alongside the canal, have been converted to an excellent off-road bike trail. Everything is close together here.

Chronologically, things went more or less as follows: First, of course, were the Indians who used the Mohawk River as a canoe link in the waterways that stretched across New York and made the Iroquois Confederacy, or Five Nations, possible. Next, European settlers used the waterways and dirt roads to migrate westward. Then came the Erie Canal, built entirely along the south shore of the Mohawk River. Just a few years later, the Utica & Schenectady built the first railroad tracing the north shore; ultimately, it and eleven other small railroads would be unified, in 1853, into the New York Central. More unpaved dirt roads came along. Then the New York West Shore & Buffalo Railroad (NYWS&B) built alongside the Erie Canal during the 1880s. Early in the 20th century, the New York Central's "Twentieth Century Limited" began service. Then the Erie Canal was relocated into the Mohawk River. Roadways were paved along both shores. The Thruway was designed during World War II and built immediately thereafter, in many paces atop the original alignment of the Erie Canal. Then, the West Shore railroad was abandoned, finally to become an off-road bike path. What a complex transportation history.

Along your route, Erie Canal Locks 10 through 20 control the Mohawk River and make it navigable. Each lock has a small park alongside — a good base point for cycling day trips.

There are also abandoned feeder canals to discover and I will offer optional tours of the two largest: the old Chenango Canal, which left Utica for Binghamton, and the Black River Canal, which stretched from Rome to Carthage.

The Chenango Canal extended from Utica south to the Susquehanna River at Binghamton, ninety-seven miles away. This canal had the remarkable summit height of 1127 feet near Bouckville. Seventy-six locks were needed to climb this "mountain" between Utica and Bouckville. Thirty-eight more locks were required to descend to Binghamton for a total of 114 locks in ninety-seven miles.

At Rome, the Black River Canal extended northward into the Adirondacks. This canal, a critical water feeder to the Erie, brought water from reservoirs and rivers in Adirondacks to the eastern summit level (426 feet above sea level) of the Erie Canal at Rome. This too was a mountain climbing canal. Its summit level was 1119 feet above sea level near Boonville. Seventy locks were required to climb from Rome to Boonville and another thirty-nine locks descended from the summit to Carthage. It took from 1836 to 1849 to complete this canal. You can find out much more about cycling along these interesting canals in Chapters 9 and 10.

All canal locks have parking and picnic sites. They are great starting or stopping points for cyclists.

There are three basic bicycling routes along the Erie Canal across the Mohawk Valley.

- First there is the Canalway Trail. Nearly complete, with a few gaps in Schenectady, Herkimer and Oneida counties, it sits primarily atop a converted rail bed and is a great way to follow the canal.
- In addition, Bike "5," which mostly follows NY 5S, is 100 percent continuous and connects all the gaps in the Canalway Trail. This is a good on-road way of cycling along the Erie Canal.
- Finally, NY 5, which follows the north shore of the Mohawk River, is also a good bicycling route with rolling hills and a wide bike lane.

So you have several choices — all three routes closely parallel each other and are never very far apart. This section will explain each one. We'll follow the Erie Canal, identify important historic sites along the way, describe how to follow the two feeder canals, and suggest some interesting loop rides. Some of the richest canal history is here in the Mohawk Valley.

Chapter 4

West to Schenectady

*If you're going to follow the Erie Canal west from Cohoes to
Schenectady, you have two options. Both of them are good so it's
not an easy decision. The simplest to follow is the Mohawk-Hudson
Bikeway, part of the Canalway Trail, which is a great paved,
off-road pathway that extends from Cohoes to Schenectady.
If you favor off-road or trail cycling, this is the choice for you.
However, it does follow the south shore of the Mohawk River and
misses some important historic Erie Canal sites on the north shore.
If you are comfortable riding on-road, I recommend following the
newly designated Mohawk Towpath Byway, a new scenic byway
that closely follows the original Erie Canal. If you have the time,
riding both is ideal and at the end of this chapter,
I will offer suggestions on how to do that.*

The Mohawk-Hudson Bikeway

You must pick up the Canalway Trail, here called the Mohawk-Hudson
Bikeway, in Cohoes. (So, if you are in Waterford, return to Cohoes.) The bikeway
can be accessed at many cross streets in Cohoes. I recommend cycling up North
Mohawk Street, climb the hill, pass the Cohoes Falls, and look for Manor Street.
Make the left. After another short climb, you will come to the Bikeway. Turn
right. You will follow this excellent trail all the way to Schenectady.

The Mohawk-Hudson Bikeway offers a beautiful ride along the Mohawk
River and the Erie Barge Canal. Town parks in Colonie and Niskayuna are
open to bicyclists. Also, there is a small park at the old Niskayuna rail depot
and one at Canal Lock 7. Most of these spots offer water and restrooms but
no food is available between Cohoes and Schenectady on this route.

This segment of Canalway Trail is built atop the roadbed of the Troy &
Schenectady Railroad (opened in 1842). This railroad was built to connect the
first railroad bridge across the Hudson River, at Troy, with the predecessors

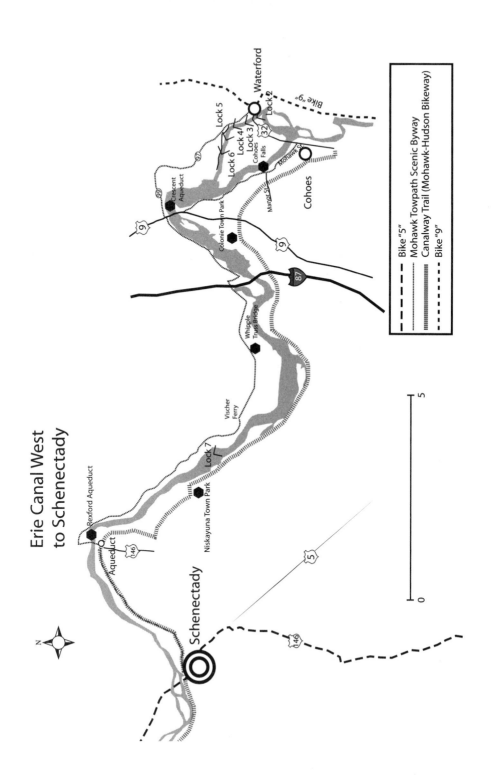

Erie Canal West to Schenectady

Waterford

Bike "9"

Lock 5
Lock 4
Lock 3
Lock 6
Cohoes Falls
32
Mohawk

Lock 2

Manor St.

Cohoes

Crescent Aqueduct

Colonie Town Park

9

9

87

Whipple Truss Bridge

Vischer Ferry

Lock 7

Rexford Aqueduct

Niskayuna Town Park

Aqueduct

146

Schenectady

146

5

N

- - - Bike "5"
.... Mohawk Towpath Scenic Byway
|||||||||||| Canalway Trail (Mohawk-Hudson Bikeway)
- - - Bike "9"

0   5

of the New York Central Railroad at Schenectady. The plan was to place Troy astride this famous railroad route. However, shortly afterward, the first railroad bridge at Albany was built — the railroad main line remained through Albany, and this little railroad to Troy became a branch line.

Travel Tip
Excellent, detailed free maps are available for both routes. See the Resource Guide.

As you travel westward, you will see the close intertwining of canal history and railroad history.

In stretches where the towpath is not available for cycling use, many of the abandoned rail lines running alongside the Erie have been converted into off-road bike paths. AMTRAK offers connecting services for bicyclists at a dozen stations along the Erie and Champlain Canals.

Up ahead, along the Mohawk-Hudson Bikeway, you'll find another small canal park just before Schenectady at Aqueduct/Rexford. Here, you can see portions of the Rexford Aqueduct which once carried the original Erie Canal across the Mohawk River to the south shore again. This was one of the longest aqueducts ever built in New York (610 feet long with 14 arches) and it's definitely worth a stop. This site is a popular spot for canoeists and scullers. There are a number of sculling boathouses and a commercial store, "The Boat House," which rents canoes and offers sculling lessons. You may spot a local boat race as you cycle past.

After stopping at Aqueduct, continue on the path into Schenectady.

Louis Rossi

Scullers training on the barge canal near the old Rexford Aqueduct.

Because the canal established such a huge traffic base and the terrain was flat, railroads came to New York very early. The first railroad charter issued in America was issued to build a rail line between Albany and Schenectady. This was in 1826, only one year after the canal was completed. Quickly, a chain of railroads was built from the Hudson to Lake Erie. In 1853, this became the famous New York Central, which is still one of America's busiest rail lines. In the late 1880s, a second railroad, the New York, West Shore & Buffalo stretched across New York. The NYWS&B was built along the "west shore" of the Hudson River, from New Jersey north toward Albany, then west along the south side of the Mohawk River toward Syracuse. Between Schenectady and Buffalo, virtually all the NYWS&B has been abandoned and much converted into rail trails.

The Mohawk Towpath Byway

This on-road ride, which closely follows to the original canal alignment, is the result of a coalition of community members (Mohawk Towpath Scenic Byway Coalition, Inc.) who have worked diligently to design, designate, and promote the route. The Mohawk Towpath Byway (MTB) has two routes to Crescent/Halfmoon. One starts from Cohoes, the other from Waterford. Food and water are available in Waterford, Halfmoon, Rexford, and Schenectady.

- From Cohoes, follow North Mohawk Street, which is on the scenic byway. The name will change to Crescent-Cohoes Road, but without any turns you will arrive in Crescent on NY 9 after about three and a-half miles of cycling. It isn't marked, but the old Erie Canal bed is on your left heading westward. At NY 9, turn right and look for a small park near the river. This is Crescent, the site of the longest aqueduct on the entire canal system (1137 feet long), which took the Erie Canal above and across the Mohawk River from Crescent to Halfmoon. After visiting the park, cross the river on NY 9. There is a small park with interpretive historical signage at both ends of the aqueduct.
- If you start from Waterford, take the scenic byway up Washington Street (which is CR 97). At the end, turn left onto CR 96, followed by a quick left onto CR 94 and another quick left onto CR 99. From Waterford, in just over four miles, you'll arrive at Halfmoon, the north side of the Crescent Aqueduct.

The Whipple Iron Truss Bridge is one of many canal sites adopted and restored by Union College students, faculty, and friends. Here, the town's summer recreation program participants make a visit.

Whether you arrived here from Cohoes or Waterford, there is only one MTB route heading west from Crescent. This is Canal Road, which heads west from the traffic light at the foot of the NY 9 bridge on the north side of the Mohawk in Halfmoon. This is the path of the Erie Canal. As you cycle along Canal Road you'll be following the route of the canal, which was used as a landfill site from 1920 to as recent as the 1970s. In just over two miles, take a right up Clam Steam Road, and then an immediate left onto Riverview Road.

Follow Riverview Road west for two miles and you'll come to the beginning of the historic Erie Canal restorations in the vicinity of Vischer Ferry. Take a careful look at the map adjacent to the restored truss bridge over the old canal. The map will point out how to get onto the old Erie Canal Towpath, which extends west for two miles. This is a dirt towpath that I recommend you try — if it is dry you can ride it on a road bike.

Iron bridges across the Erie Canal were common in the period of the early 1840s up to the opening of the New York State Barge Canal. Many bridges were removed and sold to private landowners for their use, and the state scrapped some. Students and friends of Union College rebuilt the Whipple Iron Truss Bridge, stone abutments, and approaches at Vischer Ferry with no state, federal, or town funding. It stands as a great tribute to what can be done to preserve the engineering history of the canal.

Vischer Ferry is a Greek Revival Erie Canal village circa 1840.

On the old dirt towpath trail, you'll find old Lock 19 before you come into the historic village of Vischer Ferry. If you don't want to ride atop this portion of canal towpath you can stay on Riverview Road and ride west into Vischer Ferry.

From Vischer Ferry, continue westward on Riverview Road five miles to NY 146. As you top the hill alongside the Mohawk, be sure to stop at the overlook. This looks down into the Mohawk River Gorge and you can see where the Erie Canal crossed back from the north side of the Mohawk (Rexford) to its south shore (Aqueduct). Then go left on NY 146 and cross the Mohawk River. Immediately on your left is a small park that celebrates the Erie Canal aqueduct that gave this place its name. This was another of the longest aqueducts ever built in New York (610 feet long with 14 arches).

Here at Aqueduct, the Mohawk Towpath Byway and the Mohawk-Hudson bike path merge. Regardless of which route you took from the east, I recommend that you follow the Canalway Trail the rest of the way (three miles) to downtown Schenectady.

Loops Along the Mohawk

There are seven bike-friendly bridges that cross the Mohawk River between Cohoes and Rotterdam Junction: NY 32 (Bike "9"), NY 9, NY 146, Freeman's Bridge Road, NY 5 (Bike "5"), Exit 26 Bridge (separated bikeway), and NY 103 (Bike "5"). That's seven possible crossings in an overall distance of only twenty-six river miles. That results in dozens of loop combinations between the Canalway Trail on the south shore of the Mohawk River and the on-road byway route on the north side. Take your pick — any combination is a good bike tour.

My favorite is a loop between NY 146 (Rexford-Aqueduct Bridge) and NY 32 (Broadway between Cohoes and Waterford). These bridges are about fifteen miles apart making a loop of about fifty miles a practical option. You can start anywhere on the loop — in Cohoes or Waterford on the east end, at the historic Niskayuna Depot or Vischer Ferry in the middle, at Aqueduct or Rexford on the west end, or another convenient point of your choice. Take the Mohawk-Hudson Bikeway, which extends the entire way along the south shore of the Mohawk River, in one direction and return on the on-road Mohawk Towpath Byway, which extends the entire way along the north shore of the Mohawk River. You will see all the Erie Canal sites between Cohoes and Waterford, and Rexford/Aqueduct, and many other interesting spots in between.

If fifty miles is too much, the NY 9 bridge at Crescent/Halfmoon makes two shorter loops practical. You can do a loop based on the NY 146 (Aqueduct/Rexford) Bridge and the NY 9 (Crescent/Halfmoon) Bridge one day. Then do NY 9 (Crescent/Halfmoon) and NY 32 (Waterford/Cohoes) another. The Mohawk Towpath Byway and the Mohawk-Hudson Bikeway make it easy to do a loop along the Mohawk.

The Mohawk Towpath Byway and the Mohawk-Hudson Bikeway are under separate jurisdictions and the loops go through three counties and countless cities, towns, and villages, each with its own local focus, so no unifying signs or maps exist at this time. However, the good news is that the two principal maps of the MTB and MHB are adequate and are available through the websites listed in the Resource Guide.

Chapter 5

Schenectady County

Schenectady was settled in 1661, long before the Erie Canal builders came to town. An extraordinarily historic community with good food and lodging, it is a good base for many day trips. The original canal was located beside the already 156-year-old settlement of Schenectady and today Erie Boulevard sits atop the historic canal bed. There were no locks or major canal structures here.

Visiting Schenectady

To check out Schenectady, get off the Mohawk-Hudson Bikeway at the Nott Street intersection. (Watch the traffic in this area — it's a busy crossing.) Just off Nott Street are historic neighborhoods — the "GE Plot" and the "Stockade." Traffic in these two neighborhoods is generally light and it's a short detour well worth taking. I think of Schenectady as the "Charleston of the North," with neighborhoods predating the French and Indian Wars.

Travel Tip

If you choose to ride directly through, the most direct route is to cross Nott Street, rejoin the bike path for a short distance, then follow signs (via Jay Street, Union Street, Washington Street, and State Street) to "Gateway Landing" where the pathway resumes.

First, visit Union College and the "GE Plot." Arriving from east or west, find the intersection where the bike path intersects Nott Street at grade. Turn east up Nott Street and bike through Union College, a beautifully-planned campus dating from 1790 and the first college charted in New York. You'll note the domed Nott Memorial and other handsome buildings.

Next you'll come to the "GE Plot" in a few short blocks. This small neighborhood was planned by the General Electric Company, whose headquarters were once in Schenectady, as a home site for its principal officers. Many great GE scientists, including Nobel Prize winners, lived here. There are over fifty historic homes, designed by well-known architects, including the first all-electric home (1906) and the first home to ever receive a television broadcast (1927). There is much more — to get the full story, stop at the Schenectady Museum on Nott Terrace.

The other major area to explore is the Stockade. Turn around and take Nott Street west toward Erie Boulevard. Cross Erie Boulevard and turn onto Front Street. The large factory buildings ahead of and beside you were all once part of the American Locomotive Works, or "ALCO," which was once one of the largest locomotive factories in the world.

The "Stockade" is the original Dutch trading settlement representing the furthest inland point in the Dutch colony of Nieuw Netherland. The "Stockade" dates from 1664. It was burned in 1690, during the French and Indian Wars, and subsequently rebuilt. The oldest extant house dates from 1692 and there are eight dating from the 1700s. The district, according to the National Trust for Historic Preservation, contains more old buildings on their original sites than anywhere else in the country. Be sure to see the statue of Lawrence, the Mohawk Indian who helped the Dutch settlers against the French. Take a few moments and cycle around the streets of the "Stockade."

Dick Mansfield

The Schenectady County Historical Building in the Stockade.

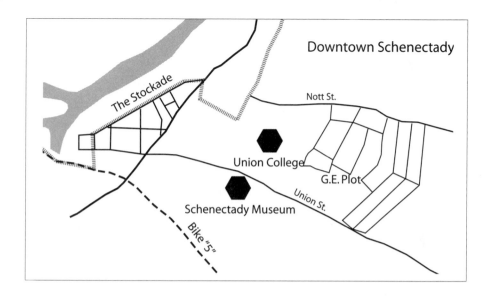

F ollowing Front Street, you'll come to State Street, which is Bike "5."
Turn right (west). In Schenectady, Bike "5" and the Canalway Trail
cross at the Western Gateway Bridge at the Mohawk River. Look carefully for
trailway signs as the paved Canalway Trail resumes along the south side of the
Mohawk and is the recommended route west. Look for the sign "Schenectady
County Gateway Landing."

Bike "5" crosses the Western Gateway Bridge and follows the north shore
of the Mohawk River. While it is not on the recommended route, if you have
the time, cross the bridge into Scotia on Bike "5" and stop at the Glen-Sanders
House, the very first building on your left, going west. It is a very short detour.
This home was a revolution in its day. Begun in 1655, it was the first home
built west of the Mohawk River. It is now a private business offering gourmet
food in the original mansion and lodging in a contemporary addition.

Going west from Schenectady, following the paved Canalway Trail on
the south shore of the Mohawk River, you will be bicycling on the original
Erie Canal towpath. You'll go past the former world headquarters of General
Electric and now the home of steam turbine production.

General Electric's economic impact on Schenectady cannot be over-stated.
Not only was this once the largest electrical shop in the world, employment
once, during World War II, was over 47,000. This is where all the electrical
equipment to operate the locks of the improved Erie Barge Canal as well
as the Panama Canal were made. Over the years, employment has withered
and with recent cutbacks, the workforce is less than 3,500. As you traverse

Restored Lock 23 (Old Erie #23) is just west of Schenectady.

the canal routes, you'll bike through dozens of other communities working to counter the decline in manufacturing jobs — and find that many are using their historic past to economic advantage.

Proceeding westbound, you'll see a restored old Erie Canal Lock (Lock 23), pass Erie Barge Canal Lock 8, and bike over your first intact original Erie Canal aqueduct. This imposing sixty-foot long, triple-arch aqueduct over Flat Stone Creek at Rotterdam Kiwanis Park was a standard design used for most small water crossings on the Erie. The three arches that support the bike path originally supported the towpath. The canal bed was below in a carefully caulked wooden trough.

Just east of Rotterdam Junction, you'll depart the trail for a section on NY 5S. Up ahead on 5S, on the south bank of the Mohawk lies the Jan Mabee farm — the oldest continuously lived-in farm in the Mohawk Valley. The nine-acre farm sits on a picturesque riverfront setting and includes the oldest house in the Mohawk Valley and a completely refurbished Dutch barn. Here, for more than 300 years, eight generations of the Mabee family were instrumental in the development of the Mohawk Valley.

Rotterdam Junction takes its name from the railroad junction you will cross at Scrafford Lane. This point marks the westernmost point of the Boston & Maine Railroad, which reached here to connect with the New York West Shore & Buffalo (NYWS&B) Railroad. You will learn more about the NYWS&B as

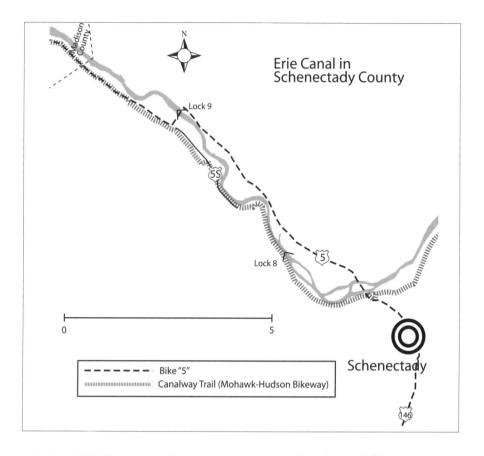

Erie Canal in Schenectady County

N

Madison County

Lock 9

5S

Lock 8

5

Schenectady

Bike "5"
Canalway Trail (Mohawk-Hudson Bikeway)

0   5

146

Jim Cassatt

The Mabee Farm is the oldest continuously lived-in farm in the Mohawk Valley.

The Erie Canal had thirty-two stone aqueducts and you will see many more as you cycle across New York. The largest was 1137 feet in length at Crescent, where nothing remains today; the smallest was just twenty-two feet at Ferguson Creek near Utica which was also demolished. In addition there were many stone culverts. You'll see Culvert 59 at Sims Store in Onondaga County, about half way to Buffalo, so there must have been more than one hundred stone culverts in all. All of the stones carefully laid to build aqueducts and locks were quarried many miles away atop the ridge or escarpment that you can see to the south. It was quite an undertaking just to get these stones to the canal construction sites.

you pedal on into Montgomery County. In Rotterdam Junction, Bike "5" again crosses the Mohawk River on NY 103 (across Erie Canal Lock 9). Follow Bike "5" westward along NY 5S.

There is a small gap in the bike path in Rotterdam Junction (Scrafford Lane). You must get back on to NY 5S. Lock 25 is found on Lock Street. The paved path resumes in Rotterdam Junction where you can ride another segment of Erie Canal towpath for about two more miles toward Pattersonville. Watch carefully for signs. This quiet segment of old canal towpath ends on NY 5S, which is Bike "5," directly adjacent to a railroad overpass which carries the former New York Central Railroad (now CSX) freight main line from the south to the north shore of the Mohawk River. Turn west (left) and in a mile and a half you'll come to the Schenectady/Montgomery County line. You must use Bike "5" heading west — there are no off-road options.

Dick Mansfield

Watch carefully for signs as the trail is constantly being changed and improved.

The Old Erie Canal from the bike path as you near Rotterdam Junction.

Dick Mansfield

For about seven miles west of Rotterdam Junction, through Pattersonville, past Erie Barge Canal Lock #9, and almost to South Amsterdam, you must follow on-road Bike "5," which is on NY 5S. This is a safe road with wide shoulders. Along the way, you'll leave Schenectady County and enter Montgomery County. Plans are underway to convert this section of railroad track you see just west of the rail overpass into a rail trail; this should be completed in 2007.

Chapter 6

Montgomery County

*The Mohawk Valley is a great place to bicycle and the forty miles
across Montgomery County offers some great options.
The Canalway Trail (paved and unpaved) is almost complete for
off-road riding. Bike "5", along NY 5S, is directly adjacent offering
a continuous, parallel on-road route. And NY 5, on the Mohawk
River's north shore, provides a cycling alternative all along the
way. Loops are very easy to find – there are sixteen bridges across
the Mohawk River from Schenectady to Utica and all are
bicycle-friendly. Not only is there easy riding in Montgomery
County, but along with some great Erie Canal history to see, the
area is host to many Mohawk Indian and colonial
and Revolutionary War sites.*

Y ou enter Montgomery County on Bike "5". After three miles, you'll
pass Erie Barge Canal Lock 10. Like at almost all locks, there is a small
park with secure parking. At Lock 10, you'll cross over the last remnants of
the West Shore railroad. Soon, this will be converted into a section of trail
that closes a gap in the Canalway Trail network between Schenectady and
Montgomery counties. After four and a-half miles more, a paved seven-
mile section of the Canalway Trail resumes on your right (look carefully.) It
continues, with paved and unpaved stretches all the way across Montgomery
County — about thirty-five miles.

In the Mohawk Valley, much of the Canalway Trail sits atop the old rail
bed of the New York West Shore & Buffalo Railroad (NYWS&B). Most of the
time, cycling off-road along the old Erie Canal in Montgomery, Herkimer and
Oneida counties, you'll be cycling on this old, historic railroad, built in the
early 1880s directly alongside the then-bustling Erie Canal.

The old New York West Shore & Buffalo Railroad near Lock 10 was once a bustling double-track railroad. It is being converted to the Canalway Trail all across the Mohawk Valley.

At Fultonville, definitely see the NYWS&B Freight House, right alongside the trail. The decorative scrollwork in the eaves still heralds the railroad's original name. At one time, this handsome scrollwork design was a standard NYWS&B feature at many dozens of freight houses which are mostly gone today. As you ride, you will notice the many freight trains moving along the north shore of the Mohawk. These trains are traveling the original New York Central mainline. Between Schenectady and Rochester, the New York Central was built to follow the Erie Canal as closely as possible.

At Amsterdam, cross the Mohawk River and visit Guy Park, the 1773 home of Guy Johnson, which is adjacent to Erie Canal Lock 11. This is a pleasant spot for a break and also an opportunity to obtain the latest tourist information from the Montgomery County Chamber of Commerce onsite. Another good stop, the home of Guy Johnson's father, Sir William Johnson, is a bit farther west.

Take care cycling through Amsterdam and cross back to the south shore as the Canalway Trail continues past Amsterdam, along the south shore of the Mohawk. It will take you directly to two important canal sites: Yankee Lock and Schoharie Crossing, both of which are interesting stopping points.

Yankee Lock (old Erie Lock #28), is one of the best preserved of the old locks. Adjacent is Putnam's Store, an authentic canal store. It's two more miles from Yankee Lock to Schoharie Crossing. You can use either the bike path (paved) or abandoned towpath (unpaved).

The Schoharie Crossing State Historic Site is the only place where you'll find all four alignments of the Erie Canal in one place. There is the original Clinton's Ditch, just four feet deep, and three successive canal enlargements. The Schoharie aqueduct is at this site. This was the third largest aqueduct

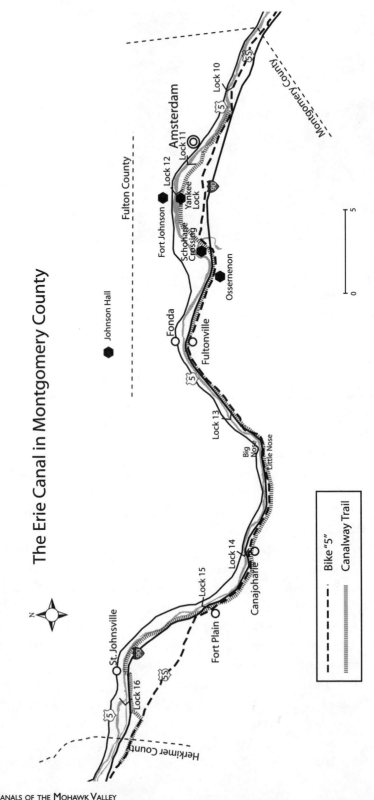

The Erie Canal in Montgomery County

Guy Park and the Lock 11 Park is a great place to stop. This home was the social center of this section of the valley for ten years before the Revolutionary war.

on the Erie Canal and today, about 300 feet of it remains. Just west of the Schoharie Creek, the paved Canalway Trail ends. Here, you can choose to stay on the trail. The trail is comprised of stone dust, except for a short, paved section through Fultonville, and extends for sixteen miles from Schoharie Crossing State park all the way to Canajoharie. Or, you can rejoin Bike "5," which is directly adjacent, atop NY 5S. The off-road trail and the on-road bike route closely follow each other all the way across Montgomery County with many interlocking points along the way. Both are good choices.

On the hill above where Schoharie Creek and the Mohawk River meet stood the Mohawk Indian palisaded village of Ossernenon. Known as the "Eastern Door" to the Iroquois Confederacy, this was the principal Mohawk Indian village. (You will see the "Western Door" in Ontario County.) In the 1640s, three French missionaries were killed here; these martyrs became the first American saints. The Auriesville Shrine located here is a major Roman Catholic religious shrine and offers insight into the powerful Iroquois Confederacy, with a distinctly religious perspective.

Yankee Lock is one of the best preserved of the old Erie Canal locks.

Visiting Johnson Hall

If you are interested in the colonial period, Indian history, and the Revolution, you should seriously consider a side trip from Fultonville to see the home of Sir William Johnson. William Johnson was a colonial of immense importance. He successfully fought for the British in the French and Indian Wars, was powerfully allied with the Indians, and was the largest landowner in the valley. In 1763 he built "Johnson Hall," a baronial house and fort. However, the Johnson heirs were Tories in the Revolutionary War and lost everything. Also losers were his ever-faithful Mohawk allies

NYS Office of Parks Recreation/Cliff Oliver Mealy

Plan a side trip to Johnson Hall – one of the most historic sites in the Mohawk Valley.

who had followed him in the Tory cause. Today his house is well preserved. Had the British won the war, I am convinced this would be America's "Mount Vernon." This is one of the most significant historical sites in the state.

The Johnson Tour: Johnson Hall, Fort Johnson and Guy (Johnson) Park

Why not connect all the Johnson Family history in one twenty-five mile loop ride? Start at Guy Park located just west of Amsterdam on NY 5.

Go west about two miles on NY 5/NY 67 to Fort Johnson and visit the earliest extant (1749) Johnson home, known today as "Old Fort Johnson." This was Sir William Johnson's principal home.

Then take NY 67 (turn right at Old Fort Johnson) and ride up a steady but easy 500+ foot climb in elevation, over about eight miles, to Johnsonville. NY 67 becomes Main Street in Johnstown. Directly on your right is a small park that contains Sir William's gravesite and a large number of historical markers that offer serious insight into the history that occurred here. Leave NY 67 (Main Street) and follow the signs to Johnson Hall (1763). You will be amazed at the history made at Johnson Hall.

Louis Rossi

You'll see the largest surviving aqueduct section at Schoharie Crossing.

The Schoharie Crossing State Park at Fort Hunter makes a good base for day trips. One day, cycle east on the Canalway Trail to Amsterdam, and return either on Bike "5" or the north side of the Mohawk River on Route 5. Another day, bike west on Bike "5" to Fort Plain and return on Route 5. Note that NY 5 is a busier highway than NY 5S (which is Bike "5"), but it has excellent shoulders and offers a different scenic perspective and access to many historic Indian sites.

Louis Rossi

Ossernenon was the chief Mohawk village, a fortified site 100 feet above the valley floor. It is now a major Roman Catholic religious shrine.

In all, it's about eleven miles from Guy Park to Johnson Hall. Consider-
ing that you'll want to visit each home, plan on leaving an extra couple of
hours for the visits. Note that each home is run by a different organization,
so call ahead for hours of operation. (If you go inside, please take off bike
shoes with cleats.)

After visiting Johnson Hall, and other historic sites in Johnsonville, go
back to NY 67, Main Street in Johnsonville. You can simply retrace your steps
to Guy Park by following NY 67, eastward from Johnstown; this is simply
the reverse of the way you came. Or, alternatively, you can head east out of
Johnstown on NY 67. In a mile, you'll come to NY 334, which bears left and
will take you to NY 5, in the Mohawk Valley, at Fonda. Follow NY 5 eastward,
through Tribes Hill, and continue on to the starting point at Guy Park.

Canajoharie and Fort Plain

You'll next come to Canajoharie,
where you might smell baby food being
processed at the old Beech-Nut plant.
Depending on what is in season, you
may smell beets, carrots, or apples.
Canajoharie has a library with an
excellent collection of American art.
The collections' building was renovated
in 2005. Canajoharie is considered the

The Canalway Trail on the old NYWS&B
route in Sprakers.

most intact Erie Canal village found in the Mohawk Valley. All of the buildings on
Church Street, many of them built with limestone, were constructed as a result
of the prosperity brought by the Erie Canal which flowed directly through the
village. In the center of town, the Canalway Trail resumes on a paved section of
the NYWS&B rail bed. The Canalway Trail will take you three miles on pavement
to the village of Fort Plain where you can visit the site of the fort. Erie Canal Lock
15 is in Fort Plain.

In Fort Plain, where the paved section of Canalway Trail ends, you can
choose to go west on an unpaved seven-mile segment of trail, with a stone
dust base, or follow Bike "5," which follows NY 5S. This stone dust segment
of Canalway Trail ends across the river from St. Johnsville where County
Route 51 crosses the Mohawk. Plans are to extend it eleven miles further
west. Both Canajoharie and Fort Plain are doing a lot to preserve their historic
downtowns and develop their canal heritage — and are worth a stop. After
Fort Plain, Bike "5" leaves the Mohawk River Valley and climbs some small
hills. Again, you'll pedal past historic markers noting the remains of Mohawk
Indian villages, such as Canawego, at hilltop locations.

The Noses

West of Fultonville, passing between the small villages of Randall and Sprakers (whether bicycling on the Canalway Trail, or on Bike "5," or boating along the Canal), you'll pass between the "Noses." Big Nose is on the north side of the Mohawk River and Little Nose on the south shore. This important passageway was a key to building the Erie Canal.

Among the many, many glacial features of New York State, this one is especially significant. Some 10,000 years ago a giant ice dam stood here, holding back the freezing waters of ancient glacial Lake Iroquois which stretched westward across what is now New York and Canada. As global warming occurred, this ice dam gave way and the waters of Lake Iroquois exploded eastward carving the passageway you see today. What had been a tall mountain "divide" between waters that flowed both east and west became a passageway for today's Mohawk River at an elevation of only about 300 feet above sea level.

The passageway of the Mohawk River between the "Noses" is not only geographically significant but also very historic. This water passageway was exploited by the first Americans and made possible the powerful Iroquois Confederacy. As noted earlier, "Ossernenon," the principal Mohawk village, and the "Eastern Door" of the symbolic "longhouse" that stretched across New York, sits just east of this gap. The builders of the Erie Canal used this passageway as a stepping stone in the ladder of locks that ultimately climbed to Lake Erie, about 570 feet above sea level. Railroad builders of the famous "water-level route," the New York Central, exploited this passageway creating the most famous railroad alignment between New York and Chicago; so too did the builders of the New York West Shore & Buffalo Railroad. America's first long-distance, limited-access highway, the Governor Thomas E. Dewey Thruway, also exploited this geological feature, long before the federal interstate highway program was conceived.

Fort Klock is just over one mile east of St. Johnsville on NY 5. (Jacob Klock was an important leader of valley revolutionaries after the death of Herkimer.) Also nearby is the Nellis Tavern, another Revolutionary War site. After seeing Fort Klock, reverse your tracks and return to River Road. Back on River Road continuing west, you'll pass Canal Lock 16 and the hamlet of Mindenville. From Mindenville, you can make a very steep climb back to Bike "5" by following Mindenville Road uphill.

For now, you must ride Bike "5" or NY 5 into Herkimer County. Very soon, a new stone dust trail will be opened on the NYWS&B right-of-way, alongside the historic Erie Canal. It is forty miles across Montgomery County.

Chapter 7

Herkimer County

*The twenty-six miles across Herkimer County offer enormous
insight into canal history and the founding of our republic. In and
around Little Falls, you'll find several sites relating to the history of
the Herkimer family. General Herkimer made his family fortune
by using slaves to haul boats around the waterfalls at Little Falls.
Through his close alliance with the Oneida Nation, he defeated
a major British invasion and gave his life in one of the most
important battles of the Revolutionary War. He planned to build a
privately-owned canal at Little Falls, which was subsequently built
by his friend Philip Schuyler. These canal locks, constructed in
1790, are the oldest and most historic in all of America.*

Heading west on Bike "5" (which is also the Canalway Trail), you'll
soon come to signs pointing you to the Herkimer Home State
Historic Site. I suggest that you stop there. The Herkimer House is four and
one-half miles from the border with Montgomery County. Turn off Bike "5"
and onto NY 169. (Bike "5" continues westward up a very steep hill along
NY 5S.) Immediately, you'll see the entrance to the Herkimer Home.

The Herkimers, of German descent, fought against the British in the
Revolution. Nicholas Herkimer, an extremely prosperous, slave-owning
farmer and trader, built this remarkable home in 1764. Although successful
as a farmer, Herkimer made his fortune by using his slaves to haul small
boats overland around the Little Falls. In 1777, he left his home to help
defeat a major British invading force and lost his life in the effort at the
Battle of Oriskany. The house is extremely well preserved and a fascinating
counterpoint to Johnson Hall. Almost identical in age, they are quite different,
although both are grand. They are truly remarkable, serving as both frontier
mansions and forts simultaneously. As loyalists to the Revolution, the
Herkimer family remained in possession of the farm for many years. You
might want to rent the old Henry Fonda, Claudette Colbert movie "Drums

The Erie Canal in Herkimer County

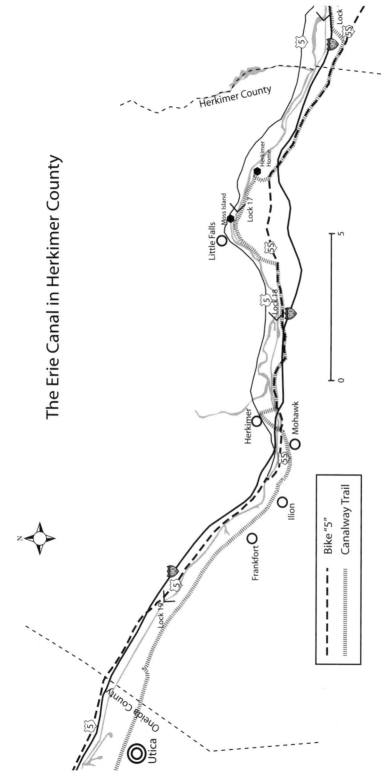

Legend:
- Bike "5"
- Canalway Trail

Labels: Herkimer County, Herkimer Home, Moss Island, Lock 17, Little Falls, Lock 18, Mohawk, Herkimer, Ilion, Frankfort, Lock 19, Oneida County, Utica, Lock

Along the Mohawk" as good preparation for this visit, in which Roger Imhoff portrays General Herkimer. Better still, for more detail, read the recently reprinted book, *Drums Along the Mohawk* by Walter Edmonds. Edmonds also authored *Rome Haul* and *Erie Water.*

Herkimer was a great American hero and should be better remembered. He was a close ally of the Oneida Nation. This alliance was critical to the Revolutionary War victories at Fort Stanwix and Oriskany, sites of which you'll cycle by in just a few miles. The Battle of Oriskany was crucial in defeating the western prong of the British plan to capture Albany and sever the colonies. Thwarting the British descent of the Mohawk was just as crucial as turning back the British descent from Lake Champlain at Saratoga in the same year. The Oriskany Battlefield site lies up ahead.

After leaving the Herkimer home, stay on NY 169 and head toward Little Falls, another Erie Canal gem. Plan to spend a little time here — there is a lot of canal history in and around the village. Little Falls got its name because it was the smaller of the two waterfalls along the Mohawk River. As noted before, the Herkimers made their fortune by using slaves to haul riverboats around these falls.

As you bike toward town along NY 169, you'll come to Canal Lock 17. You might agree that there is a certain amount of incongruity in the name Little Falls. The Mohawk River, in less than three miles, drops over forty feet as it traverses the narrow gorge. Lock 17 was built to solve this engineering challenge, replacing three locks on the 1825 Erie Canal. An imposing structure, it was the highest single lift-lock in the world for almost 100 years

Lock 17 is an imposing site. The NYWS&B is the trail on the left; Moss Island and Canal Square are on the right. NY 169 is in the foreground.

The swirling waters at the end of the last ice age scoured the deep chimney potholes near Lock 17 in the stone.

until surpassed by a lock on the Rhine-Danube canal in Germany. A smaller lock from the old Erie is nearby for comparison. Clinton's Ditch employed four locks to rise above (or descend) these falls. (These were not much larger than those of the earlier private company, which you can see later on.)

There are some glacial potholes at Lock 17 located on Moss Island that certainly justify a rest stop. Glacial potholes are formed at the edge of glaciers, where large rocks are set spinning at the base of icy waterfalls. These twirling rocks actually dig potholes in the base rock. The potholes at Little Falls are numerous and some of the largest in America. If you hunt carefully, you might see some "Little Falls Diamonds" along various outcroppings. Outstanding specimens of these unique quartz crystals are on display at the Little Falls Historical Society Museum and the Library.

To get to the potholes, carry your bike up the flight of metal steps to the top of the lock; you'll see a map showing hiking directions. It is only a short hike, climbing steeply up over rocks with few handholds. Ask the locktender for directions if you are unsure.

Now, cycle west less than a mile on the paved service road along the barge canal to Little Falls. You'll arrive at Benton's Landing near Canal Place.

You'll find still more historic markers and sites describing the complex canal history at this point.

Here, in 1795, a private company, the Western Inland Navigation Company, completed a series of small locks to bypass the falls. Archeological excavations have unearthed old lock and canal sites just west of Canal Place along Elizabeth Street. General Philip Schuyler, whose home you might have seen in Albany, was a founder of the company that built this small canal.

Although economically unsuccessful, the Western Inland Canal demonstrated the potential of water transportation.

Also in Little Falls, you will see the main line of the old New York Central again. Still one of the busiest railroads in America, the New York Central emerged from a series of smaller short rail lines in 1853. At Little Falls, the railroad was built as the Utica & Schenectady, opening in 1836. If you follow NY 169 across the Mohawk River into Little Falls, there is a small historic marker identifying the site of one of the worst train wrecks on the New York Central Railroad. Here, in 1940, the Lake Shore Limited was derailed at a sharp curve, killing thirty-one passengers. The curve was later straightened.

As you can tell, there is a lot to see in this small area. Additionally, a short, paved rail trail (over the NYWS&B) begins at Finks Basin Road, runs right beside Lock 17, and continues to NY 167. Since everything is in a small area, you will find your way easily.

Little Falls is typical of most Mohawk Valley communities — it struggles against the economic decline that began shortly after World War II. However, the village is doing a great job celebrating its rich canal heritage and in turn, revitalizing the downtown area.

Each August, Little Falls holds a weeklong Canal Days celebration. There are lectures, boat trips, historic tours and the Canal Classic bicycle race. This race, while on a hilly course, is very welcoming of novice racers.

Little Falls is another good base for an overnight stay with good lodging and food choices and plenty of canal history to explore.

After Little Falls, take NY 167 across the canal and you will reconnect with the Canalway Trail, which rejoins NY 5S (Bike "5") in just a few miles.

There are still a few important things to see before leaving Herkimer County. Two miles along on Bike "5" is Lock 18 at Johnsonburg. Its well-marked entrance looks like a driveway, which it is, but try it and you'll come alongside the old Erie Canal again as the access road rides on top of the old towpath. After visiting this lock, less than two miles further is a very important historic site directly alongside Bike "5." This is the Fort Herkimer Church built

Little Falls was once noted for its woolen mills and small factories, and was the region's cheese and agricultural marketing center.

in 1730. This is the original Herkimer family homestead and site of General Herkimer's birth. The stone church served as a fortress in conjunction with the actual wooden fort that was just a few hundred feet further west. The site of that fort is now a small roadside park alongside the Mohawk River. To me, this stone church conveys a strong sense of how life was in pre-Revolutionary, frontier America.

Continue west past the villages of Herkimer, Mohawk, and Ilion. Bike "5" bypasses each of them, but feel free to explore them if you have time. The Remington Firearms Museum at Ilion, just off Bike "5," might be of interest to you. Ilion is the home of Remington Arms, and the museum chronicles the history of the firm, which built bicycles in the 1800s, and which has been at this site since 1816.

At NY 51, in Ilion, Bike "5" turns north and crosses the Mohawk River and turns west onto NY 5. Follow the signs toward Utica. This is a well-signed bike route. You'll cycle for a while right alongside the old New York Central mainline. Look for Lock 19, as it is a nice picnic or rest area. Notice how the railroad crosses almost directly in front of the lock. Back on Bike "5," it is just four more miles from Lock 19 to the end of Herkimer County.

If you were to cycle directly across Herkimer County on Bike "5," it would be a fast, twenty-six mile ride. Following the many detours I've recommended will lengthen your trip accordingly.

The off-road unpaved Canalway Trail should be open between Little Falls and Ilion early in 2007, and from Ilion to Utica by 2009. Until these segments are available, you should follow Bike "5," which can be busy.

Chapter 8

Eastern Oneida County

In Oneida County you'll find some of America's most important Revolutionary War sites. There are also some striking Erie Canal remains as well as two of the largest feeder canals, the Chenango Canal (Chapter 9) and Black River Canal (Chapter 10). It is eighteen miles between the Herkimer County line and Fort Stanwix in Rome and another seventeen miles to the Madison County line. That's the fast way on Bike "5" following the north shore of the Mohawk River. Seeing the sites along the way will add many miles.

At the Oneida County border, you will be on Herkimer Street on the north side of the city of Utica. Utica, unlike the cities to the east such as Schenectady, Troy and Albany, owes its development to the completion of the Erie Canal. This is much the same for Syracuse, Rochester, and Buffalo, all of which grew rapidly as a result of the canal. As such, Utica was not an important site in the wars of the 18th and 19th centuries. A small earthen and wood fort, called Fort Schuyler, was built in 1758 just east of today's Amtrak station. Unfortunately, nothing remains.

If you wish to tour the historic, but closed, Chenango Canal, go to the next chapter. To head westward along the Erie, you face two choices — a newly opened segment of Canalway Trail or on-road Bike "5." To pick up the Canalway Trail, follow directional signing to the Utica Harbor, which is just west of Genesee Street. From the harbor (that's the Erie Canal "harbor" in Utica), a stretch of Canalway trail extends west just shy of six miles to NY 291 near Oriskany. Alternatively, you can ride on-road on Bike "5" from Utica to this very same point; Bike "5" follows NY 49 to NY 291. So, if you've arrived at NY 291 by Canalway Trail or Bike "5," you must cycle on-road, westward on NY 69, which carries the Bike "5" shield. Go west. In just two miles, as you enter the village of Oriskany, you'll cross over Oriskany Creek. If you stop and

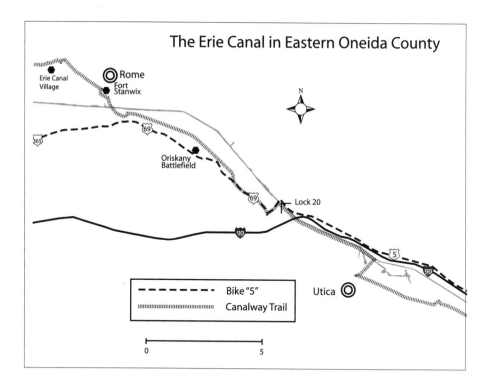

The Erie Canal in Eastern Oneida County

Legend:
- - - - - - - Bike "5"
IIIIIIIIIIIIIIIIIIIIIIIIIIIIIIII Canalway Trail

Visiting Utica

The city of Utica offers some interesting places to visit. To do so, you need to leave Bike "5." Take either Genesee Street, which is a busy arterial, or a short segment of exclusive bikeway located about a mile ahead. The bikeway will take you along the Erie Barge Canal to Utica's Barge Canal docks. These are worth seeing because, at one time, every inland city along the barge canal had a terminal like this. Remember that these docks linked these small places with the cities of the Great Lakes and Atlantic Seaboard.

Look carefully for the entrance to the bikeway; it is adjacent to a highway off ramp, across from Flanagan Road. The bike path ends on Genesee Street so you will have to ride the busy street into downtown.

The Amtrak Station is unique in that it is the only one of the few great urban terminals of the New York Central to be preserved and used. It is in excellent condition and contains a bookstore with many books of interest to the transportation historian. Further along (south) Genesee Street are the Munson-Williams-Proctor Institute and the Oneida County Museum. Along Memorial Parkway are a number of statues of famous people. Two are from the American Revolution: General Wilhelm Baron Von Steuben and Brigadier General Casimir Pulaski. None of the original Erie Canal remains to be seen in Utica today. It all lies beneath modern highways.

look just a few feet to the south side of the highway crossing, you'll see ruins of an old Erie Canal Aqueduct. The Oriskany Creek Aqueduct was a four-arch stone span 105 feet long. Another unpaved section of off-road Canalway Trail resumes just after the village; look for it on your right. You can take this off-road trail, or stay on NY 69, Bike "5," and head west toward Rome, about six and a half miles away. But along the way, in just two miles, you'll come to the site of the Battle of Oriskany. Be sure to stop here.

The Oriskany Battlefield Historical Site is the location of one of the most important battles of the Revolution. It was here that the Americans stopped the British invasion of the Mohawk Valley and thwarted plans to link up with the invading force under General Burgoyne. The success here affected not only the Battle of Saratoga, but also eventually, the outcome of the war. Here, General Herkimer was mortally wounded. Reenactments take place every August 6th.

The Oriskany Battlefield is right next to the Canalway Trail and Bike "5."

After your visit, do not retrace your steps. Continue west on NY 69, Bike "5," or the Canalway Trail and follow the on-road Canalway Trail signs northwest into the City of Rome. You'll ride up Martin and Mill Streets — be careful with the traffic along this short stretch. This will bring you to Fort Stanwix.

Downtown Rome was "modernized" with major urban renewal so the rebuilt Fort Stanwix sits there as a historic island in a sea of cars and highways. Fort Stanwix marks the western end of the Mohawk River. From here it was a short portage of only one mile to the Wood Creek, which extended into Oneida Lake and on to Lake Ontario. This

The British invasion of the Mohawk Valley was turned back here at the Battle of Oriskany. The monument was built from limestone blocks removed from old Erie Canal locks.

ancient path, used by Indians for centuries, was an important strategic route during the Revolutionary War. Fort Stanwix, originally built in 1758, choked

Visitors to Fort Stanwix can watch a military drill demonstration and experience 18th-century soldier life.

Fort Stanwix National Monument.

off access from Lake Ontario. The successful defense of this fort prevented the British from entering the Mohawk River Valley. Had they been able to do so, the possibility of a successful link-up with General Burgoyne's troops moving south down the Champlain Valley toward Saratoga was very real. The victory at Fort Stanwix along with the defeat of the British at Saratoga, were the turning points in the Revolutionary War.

Here, at the headwaters of the Mohawk, you are leaving the western extent of the lands officially under the British crown. These headwaters mark the farthest possible westernmost extent of the original claim of the colony of Nieuw Netherland. From here, westward, you enter the sovereign lands of the Haudenosaunee. (Haudenosaunee means *People of the Long House.*) The Haudenosaunee note that they operate under the oldest continually operating form of confederated government, called the Grand Council of the Haudenosaunee. International treaty laws are quite tricky and far too complex to explain here, but the Dutch, French, and British always recognized the Haudenosaunee as an independent nation adjacent to the colony of New York. As a result, under American Law, the Haudenosaunee are quite different than other Indian tribes. This legal "confusion," (it is not confusing to the Haudenosaunee) persists to this day resulting in bitter land disputes you will see evidence of in central and western New York.

Although from a military perspective the American Revolution in the Mohawk Valley was a success, the population fared poorly from the almost constant warfare. According to historians, less than a third of the population remained after the "successful" conclusion of the many wars in the valley. Many were dead. Many settlers were Tories who fled to Canada for their lives. The American Revolution destroyed the power of the Iroquois Confederation. The Mohawks and Seneca's, the two most powerful tribes, allied with the British. The smaller Oneida tribe joined the revolutionary cause. The Onondagas and Cayugas tried to remain neutral and the central fire was symbolically extinguished.

If you wish to follow the historic Black River Canal, go to Chapter 10. If you wish to head west, you have two options. You can return to Bike "5" (NY 365) and follow it to NY 31 which will connect to the Erie Canal State Park in about fifteen miles. A better choice is to search out the eastern trail head to the state park about three miles west of Fort Stanwix at the Erie Canal Village. You need to follow NY 46/69 (Erie Boulevard) to get there. This is a busy street, but Liberty Street runs parallel and can be a safer ride. This will open up thirty-six miles of great riding on the Old Erie Canal State Park towpath. (Chapter 11)

Classical Names in Upstate New York

You have now cycled through Ilion, Utica, and Rome. The Black River Canal extended from Rome to Carthage. Continuing west, you will pass through Verona, Mycenae, Manlius, Syracuse, Galen, Cato, Greece, Egypt, Macedon, Medina and other place names from the classical world. Why? The answer to this mystery arises out of the many wars which took place in upstate New York. Constant warfare with the Indians and between the British and French kept colonial New York limited to the Hudson Valley and a few parts of the eastern Mohawk Valley. Opening the territory west of Rome for safe settlement coincided with the founding of the American republic. With an exuberance that befit both events, people in the late 1700s used names from classical Rome and Greece to indicate the promise they saw in their new communities and the new republic.

Chapter 9

The Chenango Canal

The ninety-seven mile Chenango Canal is another of the great,
unexplored bike routes in upstate New York. This canal was built
between 1833-1836 and extended south from the Erie Canal at
Utica to the Susquehanna River at Binghamton.
The main purpose of the canal was to haul Pennsylvania coal
and local lumber and goods up to the Erie Canal. Along the way it
passed through Clinton, Oriskany Falls, Solsville, Bouckville
(the summit at 1127 feet above sea level), and on through
Earlsville, Sherburne, Norwich, Oxford, and Greene. These are
picturesque villages worth visiting today.

One hundred and sixteen locks were required to climb up to the summit level near Bouckville and descend down to the Susquehanna River at Binghamton. In the first twenty miles or so, going south from Utica, seventy-six locks were required to climb from the 423 foot elevation of the Erie Canal to the summit level of 1127 feet — a 704-foot climb! The summit level stretched from Solsville through Bouckville and south toward Hamilton. Then, the canal more slowly descended alongside the Chenango River to the Susquehanna River at Binghamton, requiring just twenty-one locks along the way.

Reaching the Susquehanna River was important as it enabled raw materials from Pennsylvania (particularly coal and lumber) to move north into New York. Because of unreliability in the water levels of the Susquehanna, the construction of yet another canal, the Chenango Canal Extension was authorized in 1838. It extended alongside the Susquehanna River's south shore, from Binghamton toward the Pennsylvania border about twelve miles away. Portions were opened, but the extension was never completed. Construction on the extension was suspended in 1872. Shortly thereafter, the Chenango Canal was closed.

As you plan to cycle along the route of the Chenango Canal, put your mind in exploratory mode. The basic route of the Chenango Canal is pretty easy to follow, but finding old canal structures requires some hunting. Generally, NY 12B and NY 12 follow the canal; here and there, local county roads follow it more closely. These are all pretty good roads for road cycling. You also may want to explore some of the segments of towpath by mountain bike or hybrid.

While the whole route totals about one hundred miles, there are many out-and-back segments that are wonderful day trips. One such loop from the Erie Canal at Utica would be to follow the recommended Chenango Canal route to Hamilton, spend the night, and then return.

The Chenango Canal left the Erie Canal in Utica in the vicinity of Genesee Street. In the city, it now lies under a major arterial highway (NY 5, NY 8, NY 12) and little remains to be found. From Utica, head south on Genesee Street, which is safe for cycling outside commuter hours, and you'll pass the Munson-Williams-Proctor Institute (310 Genesee Street) and Oneida County Historical Society (1608 Genesee Street). Follow Genesee Street past NY 12 and turn onto NY 12B heading toward Clinton. NY 12B parallels the old canal route through Clinton, Franklin Springs, Deansboro and Oriskany Falls. It was along this twenty-mile stretch that seventy-six locks were built to raise the canal about 706 feet. There is not much to be found — a historic marker here or there, but the riding is pretty.

> **Travel Tip**
>
> Unlike the Erie Canal, the Chenango Canal property was largely sold off and nearly one hundred and twenty-five years later, much has been lost, or is hidden and not yet recovered. Because of this, there are not many off-road (towpath) cycling opportunities along the Chenango Canal. There's a lot of volunteer interest and activity in restoring the canal route so other segments of the old towpath or paralleling rail beds should be opened for cycling in the future. At present, following the Chenango Canal is for on-road cyclists but the riding is safe and fun.

Louis Rossi

Volunteers have worked weekends to establish a five-mile hiking/biking trail here at the summit.

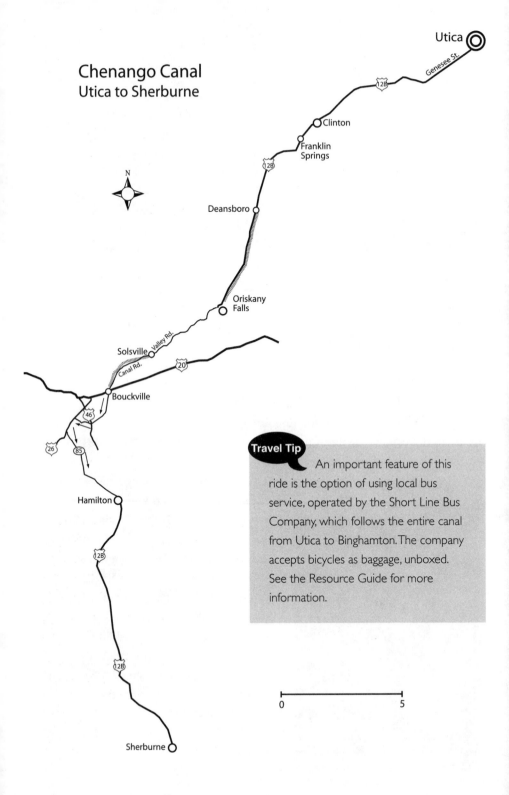

Chenango Canal
Utica to Sherburne

Utica

Genesee St.

12B

Clinton

Franklin
Springs

12B

Deansboro

Oriskany
Falls

Solsville   Valley Rd.

Canal Rd.

20

Bouckville

46

26   85

Hamilton

12B

12B

Sherburne

N

Travel Tip An important feature of this ride is the option of using local bus service, operated by the Short Line Bus Company, which follows the entire canal from Utica to Binghamton. The company accepts bicycles as baggage, unboxed. See the Resource Guide for more information.

0   5

From Oriskany Falls to Hamilton (twelve miles), through Solsville and Bouckville, lies the summit of the canal. This is one of the most scenic, rural, and genuinely attractive canal segments in all of New York. Leave NY 12B in Oriskany Falls and follow Valley Road to Solsville. The wetlands alongside the road and the beautiful ponds you see today are the old canal bed. At Solsville, turn onto Canal Road and follow it to Bouckville. Look carefully for canal

A short stretch of rail-to-trail along Oriskany Creek begins at Deansboro.

sites along the way; there is a small stone aqueduct recently restored.

Volunteers have restored a stretch of trail from NY 46 to Bouckville, going towards Solsville. This five-mile section was called the "summit" because it was the highest point of the canal 165 years ago. As you can see from the photo, the trail is dirt and grass so the quiet, rural farm roads that lie alongside the canal will offer even better cycling for road bikes.

The five-mile Summit Trail is great for hiking or mountain biking.

On the corner of Canal Road and Route 20 you'll come to the Chenango Canal Cottage, a restored small cottage and walkway along the Chenango Canal in Bouckville open to the public. The Cottage features pictures of the canal as well as a brief history and insight into the days of its use in transporting goods from Pennsylvania to the Erie Canal.

As you stop, you might picture the sixty stagecoaches a day that once rumbled through this intersection along the old Cherry Valley route, with many travelers staying in the nearby canal hotels, including what is now the Bouckville Antique Corner. Across the street is an 1847 cobblestone landmark.

Continue straight across US 20 onto Canal Road and you'll soon come to NY 46. Turn right onto Pecks Road. You'll cross another grassy stretch of canal towpath just ahead. Then, after Pecks Road ends at NY 26, turn left, then left again onto CR 85. Follow CR 85 (Smith Road) into Hamilton, where it rejoins NY 12. Hamilton, the home of Colgate University, is a beautiful village with many historic buildings and several options for food and drink.

Louis Rossi

The Chenango Canal Cottage in Bouckville is packed with information on the canal.

From Hamilton, the best way to follow the Chenango Canal is to stay on NY 12B until it joins with NY 12, then stay on NY 12 all the way to Greene, (forty-five miles from Hamilton). You'll pass through Middleport (guess how it got its name), Earlville, Sherburne, Norwich, Oxford and Greene. A large number of historic markers note unique and interesting canal history all along NY 12 in Chenango County.

You can search for old canal sites in local villages along the way — keep your eye out for street names such as...Chenango Street... Canal Street...Lock Street...Towpath Street... Water Street...and so forth. These are hints for a successful canal explorer. You'll find these local villages to be historic and attractive with good food and lodging choices.

Many historic markers along the way point out facts and figures about the canal.

The Village of Greene has a North Canal Street and a South Canal Street. Just on the south edge of town, on NY 12, is a historic marker identifying the location of a major aqueduct which carried the Chenango Canal from the west side of the Chenango River to its eastern bank. The ruins of this aqueduct are worth stopping to see.

The remains of the Greene Aqueduct, on the south side of the village, are worth a stop.

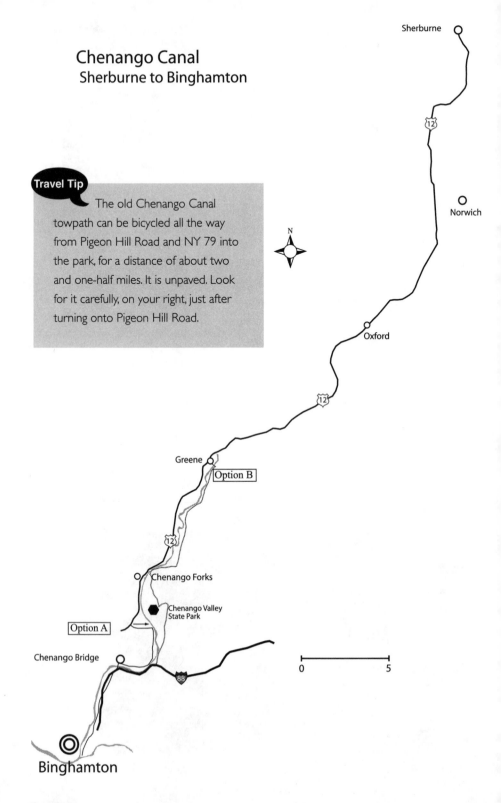

Chenango Canal
Sherburne to Binghamton

Sherburne

12

Norwich

N

Travel Tip

The old Chenango Canal towpath can be bicycled all the way from Pigeon Hill Road and NY 79 into the park, for a distance of about two and one-half miles. It is unpaved. Look for it carefully, on your right, just after turning onto Pigeon Hill Road.

Oxford

12

Greene

Option B

12

Chenango Forks

Chenango Valley State Park

Option A

Chenango Bridge

88

0   5

Binghamton

Just south of the village of Greene, the canal this aqueduct carried crossed over to the east side of the Chenango River. The route options get a bit more complicated so here are your choices:

- **Option A.** To take a direct route to Binghamton, stay on NY 12 for about twenty miles, or
- **Option B.** To follow the canal closely, cross the Chenango River at Greene and follow local roads.

Option A: Approaching Binghamton on NY 12/Bike "17," two and one-half miles south of Chenango Forks, you'll see a sign for Bike 4, a locally-designated bike route, which leaves NY 12 and turns left. This is Kattelville. Take Bike 4, (River Road) into Binghamton; it is much safer than Bike "17."

Option B: At Greene, cross the Chenango River on NY 41, immediately turn right onto Water Street (CR 32) and follow it to NY 79 (NY Bike "17"). Turn right. At Pigeon Hill Road you should turn left and you'll come to Chenango Valley State Park. Enter the park; inside there is an old section of old towpath open for cycling and an old lock (#107).

Now, from Chenango Valley State Park, follow NY 369 south to Port Crane. In Port Crane, you'll find a Towpath Street, a Lock Street, and a Canal Street. Now comes the real challenge — you must bicycle one exit (1.75 miles from Exit 3 to Exit 2) on the wide-shoulders of I-88! This is technically illegal, but it is "tolerated" by police since there is simply no other route. Many cyclists use this route. If this bothers you, you can pedal back to NY 79 (Bike 17) and go west to NY 12 at Chenango Forks.

From Port Crane southward, Bike "4" closely follows the route of the Chenango Canal through Port Dickinson and down State Street in Binghamton (which was the route of the Chenango Canal) and will take you directly to Confluence Park, an attractive small park on the Susquehanna River in downtown Binghamton. Interesting historical markers describe this as where the old Chenango Canal entered the Susquehanna River.

Enjoy this on-road ride! This is an especially beautiful part of New York.

The Susquehanna River in Binghamton makes a great starting or stopping place for canal exploration by bike.

Chapter 10

The Black River Canal

Touring the Black River Canal will take you through great scenery and on into the Saint Lawrence River Valley in the Western Adirondacks. It is a great on-road bike ride which you can do as a loop from the Erie Canal (follow the directions to Boonville and the "The Flight of Locks") or a multi-day extended bike trip into the St. Lawrence River Valley.

At Rome, the very important Black River Canal extended north into the Adirondacks. This canal was a critical water feeder to the Erie, bringing water from reservoirs and rivers in Adirondacks to the Erie's "summit" level (426 feet above sea level) at Rome. The Black River Canal was another "mountain climbing" canal. Its summit level was 1119 feet above sea level near Boonville. Seventy locks were required to climb from Rome to Boonville and another thirty-nine locks descended from the summit at Boonville to Carthage. It took from 1836 to 1849 to complete the construction of this canal.

Following the Black River Canal on-road is fairly simple. The Black River Canal extended north from the Erie Canal in Rome. It began in the vicinity of Fort Stanwix. Today, in the city of Rome, the canal route lies beneath Black River Boulevard, NY 46, which you should follow for about two and one-half miles to the city line. Black River Boulevard can be a busy street and if traffic concerns you, use one of the quieter, paralleling side streets to the west. Many cyclists prefer riding George Street until it connects with NY 46 near the outskirts of Rome. Once outside of Rome, NY 46 and the other on-road routes you'll follow are good, safe bicycling roadways. NY 46 is directly adjacent to the canal between Rome and the summit-level at Boonville, a distance of twenty-five miles. Along the way, a stretch of off-road cycling is possible along the old towpath. Then, north of Boonville, NY 12 traces the canal from Boonville through Lyons Falls to Lowville, and NY 26 from Lowville to Carthage, another 50 miles, for a total of nearly 75 miles. Arriving at Carthage, the Saint Lawrence River Valley beckons.

The Black River Canal

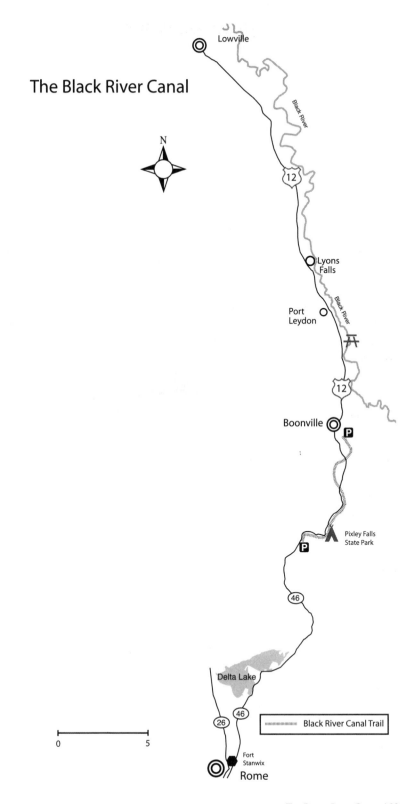

Lowville

Black River

N

12

Lyons
Falls

Black River

Port
Leydon

12

Boonville P

Pixley Falls
State Park

P

46

Delta Lake

46

26

▦▦▦▦▦▦ Black River Canal Trail

0   5

Fort
Stanwix

Rome

To begin, follow NY 46 northward out of Rome. The river you are following is the Upper Mohawk River. Just six miles from Rome is Delta Lake State Park. Delta Lake is a major reservoir for the Erie Canal. The large dam you see was built in 1908. The old Village of Delta and the original Black River Canal lie beneath the lake's waters. Continuing north on NY 46, keep your eye out for old locks of the Black River Canal. There were seventy-one stone locks between Rome and Boonville. These were necessary to climb the 700 or so feet in altitude to reach the 1119-foot

Dick Mansfield

The canal towpath is open for mountain biking/hiking for 7.5 miles.

summit level at Boonville. As you bike up NY 46, perhaps the best (or toughest depending on your perspective) climb alongside any single canal segment in New York, you'll get a great appreciation for the canal builders who raised and lowered 100-150 ton canal boats up and down this same climb. As you reach the summit, you'll have climbed out of the Mohawk River Valley and into the upper reaches of the Black River, which flows north into Lake Ontario and the Saint Lawrence River.

Off-road bikers should look for the canal towpath which is open for cycling. It begins just after you enter the Town of Ava (look for the sign) then continues alongside NY 46, through Pixley Falls State Park (good campsite) and into Boonville, for a total distance of about six and one-half miles. This is not a paved trail, but it is kept in pretty good condition; give it a try. In the winter it is a good cross-country ski trail.

Lock 70 controlled the south end of the summit-level and Lock 71 the north end. As Boonville was the summit of canal waters, it was critical that canal builders supplied enough water to keep the canal filled. Five Adirondack reservoirs, as far as twenty-five miles away, provided the water that kept the canal filled so boats could travel "down," south toward Rome or north toward Carthage.

Louis Rossi

Heading north from Boonville, the canal began an immediate and rapid descent. A historical marker alongside NY 12 identifies the site of Lock 71. Heading north from Boonville, NY 12 sits atop the old canal bed for several miles. Be watchful: in just four miles, you'll either pass through or pass alongside the remains of at least ten stone locks. Then you'll come to a "rest stop" in the median of NY 12, where five well-preserved locks can be seen. This flight of locks is an awesome site.

Lock 71 in Boonville was the summit of the canal.

At this point, you have seen the most important Black River Canal sites. If you turn back to Rome it makes a lengthy out-and-back ride of nearly 60 miles.

If you want to continue north, just stay on NY 12 and you'll pass through the village of Port Leyden (can you guess how it got its name?) and in just ten miles from Boonville, you'll arrive in Lyons Falls. To find canal sites here, you need to get

Louis Rossi

The park north of Boonville on NY 12 is a great place to look at canal structures.

off NY 12 and enter the village. Here, at Lock 109, after descending twenty-five locks and descending about 300 feet from the summit level, the Black

River Canal "ended." It "ends" in a unique way in that the separate channel section entered the Black River itself.

The most direct route to follow the canal north from Lyons Falls is to get back on NY 12 and ride it into Lowville. From Lowville, you should ride NY 26 to Carthage. There are no canal sites to see, but this is beautiful farm country and the Black River itself makes for excellent canoeing.

It may seem kind of odd that the Black River Canal came to an end in Carthage. Carthage was an important mill town, but hardly seems like a logical terminus. Indeed, there were plans to extend the Black River Canal further north. One plan was to follow the Black River itself, through Watertown and on into Lake Ontario, only thirty miles away. A more ambitious plan would have left Carthage and crossed over to the headwaters of the Oswegatchie River and follow it to Ogdensburg, on the Saint Lawrence, sixty miles away. These were pretty flat routes and a canal would have been pretty efficient on these alignments. But by the time these decisions had to be made, the railroad era had arrived. It was recognized by canal builders that the time for expanding the system of New York canals had come to an end. While these proposed canal routes were never developed, they offer great cycling opportunities through the rich, rolling farmlands of the St. Lawrence River Valley.

The Black River Canal remained in service a lot longer than most feeder or lateral canals. This is in part because it was so well built (as the excellent condition of the old locks still demonstrates today), in part because freight traffic levels were good, and most importantly because the section from Boonville to Rome fed Adirondack waters to the long-level of the Erie Canal.

The canal north of Boonville was closed in 1900 after forty-five years of active service. The canal south of Boonville remained in service until construction of Delta Reservoir blocked its route. But, although closed to navigation, it was maintained

For another thirty-seven miles, the Black River itself comprised the canal. No other 19th century canal in New York used a navigable river. There were just two control dams and locks, which created a reasonably stable "slack water" river bringing navigation all the way to Carthage.

and continues to bring water from the high reservoirs in the Adirondacks down to Delta Reservoir and today's Erie Canal.

Dick Mansfield

The Black River was the canal from Lyons Falls to Carthage.

The Canals of Central New York

*Fort Stanwix guards the westernmost headwaters of
the Mohawk River. From here, the Mohawk River bends
northwards into the Adirondacks. Historically, you are
leaving the lands of the Mohawks and entering the lands of
the Oneidas. From here, water flow was no longer toward the
Hudson River and the Atlantic, but toward the west and north
— into and through Oneida Lake and ultimately into
Lake Ontario and the Saint Lawrence River.*

West of Rome, the builders of the original Erie Canal chose a
land-locked route that went across flat, low-lying marshy lands.
This permitted building the longest, flattest stretch of the original Erie Canal
— over 50 miles without a lock. As you bike westward, you will cross some
of New York's flattest topography. This made building the Erie Canal easier,
but it also meant crossing New York's worst swamplands. This lowland is
the bottom of an ancient glacial lake called Lake Iroquois. The southern
shores of that lake are the hilltops you see to your south. Lake Iroquois
was so big, extending over much of the eastern Great Lakes that in relation,
today's giant Lake Ontario is a mere puddle. When the ice cap melted
enough to permit the waters of Lake Iroquois to spill out, the resultant flood
was so instantaneous and large that it altered the drainage pattern of eastern
North America. No longer would the Great Lakes drain southward through
the Mississippi River but northeast into the Saint Lawrence River.

The "Ononodaga" enters Barge Canal Lock 24 at Baldwinsville.

In the 20th century, the builders chose an entirely new alignment when they built the modern Erie Barge Canal. It was relocated quite a ways north of the old Erie, back to old Haudenosaunee routes, into navigable rivers. That's why the longest, unspoiled sections of the original Erie Canal unfold here in Central New York. The present barge canal system uses Oneida Lake and the Oneida and Seneca Rivers to extend westward. The old canal alignment lies well south. Because today's canal is so separate from the historic canal, this portion of our tour lets us see the Erie Canal as it was in the 19th century, for the most part, unchanged. Today, most of this original canal route is open for off-road cycling atop the original Erie towpath in the Old Erie Canal State Historic Park.

Bike "5" follows NY 31, which kind of splits the distance and lies in between both canal routes. The next two chapters will describe how to follow the original Erie Canal, how to use Bike "5" to get close to canal sites, and offer some options.

There were many feeder canals that extended the reach of the original Erie to nearby communities and/or brought water to the Long Level. Eleven feeders and connections to the Erie Canal were built in Central New York.

The Fort Stanwix area was the westernmost limit of early 17th century exploration by Dutch traders, and probably represented the edge of New Netherland. The French considered this their colony — "New France" — as the river drainage was all part of "their" Saint Lawrence River basin. The Haudenosaunee certainly did not concur, were bitter foes of the French and were close allies to the Dutch and subsequently the British. After British takeover of New Netherland in 1664, the ownership of these lands became a bit grayer. By-and-large, the British considered these lands as part of a neighboring sovereign nation — the Five Nations and then Six Nations. Only after the Revolution were all these lands claimed to be part of the new State of New York. It's quite a complicated story and land disputes continue in the 21st century. You very well may see evidence of these 400-year-old land disputes as you bicycle along these ancient trade corridors.

Jim Cassatt

The builders chose an entirely new alignment when they built the modern Erie Barge Canal.

Chapter 11

Western Oneida and Madison Counties

The Old Erie Canal State Historic Park stretching from Rome to Syracuse has some terrific canal historic sites to see. We will start by riding west from Rome and getting on the old towpath which begins at the Erie Canal Village. You very well may want to visit the village, a reconstructed 19th century community with three museums and a wealth of historical artifacts and information. You can, in season, catch a mule-towed canal boat ride or excursion train. There is a modest admission fee.

I t is an easy ride for the thirty-six miles to Syracuse. As this is the original towpath, you'll find surfaces of stone dust and grass with a few rough patches. In good weather, these surfaces are fine for cycling; after wet periods, they can be soft or muddy and sometimes impassable. But all along the route you'll see quiet, local roads that closely parallel the old towpath; feel free to use these roads if trail conditions are poor or if you want to make faster time. While there are no locks, there are three well-preserved old aqueducts that still carry water from old Erie Canal reservoirs to the summit of today's barge canal.

This section, called the Long Level, is unique in that it had no locks for over fifty miles. The original Erie Canal builders achieved a totally flat alignment between Lock 46 just west of Utica, and Lock 47 in Syracuse. Builders of the modern Erie Barge Canal achieved an even longer Long Level — you'll see that stretch further west. Remarkably, this stretch you are riding along, the oldest section of Erie Canal, although closed to commercial boat traffic, is still in use. It brings water from reservoirs located in the hills to the south to the summit of the Erie Barge Canal west of Rome.

If you have been riding along the Erie Canal since Albany you are, just now, arriving at the canal's starting point. From a canal perspective, it is important to note that it all began here, on July 4, 1817, when the digging began near Rome.

Why here? This was not an easy place to reach in those days. Using the old politician's trick, still very much in use today, Governor Clinton did not begin digging his "ditch" from one or both ends; he began in the middle. Of course, getting started in the middle, then, as now, meant that you had to complete everything to have a useful canal. Unless the entire canal was finished, the middle sections would prove useless. Moreover, as the middle sections were the most level (flattest), more work could be accomplished quickly.

About ten miles into the ride, near State Bridge, you will ride a two-mile section on the road. Bike "5" intersects and continues west along NY 31 across Madison County. Unless you are in a hurry, don't use Bike "5." Instead, follow the Old Erie Canal Historic State Park trail. While the thirteen-mile trip across Madison County on this section of Bike "5" (NY 31) makes for fast riding and takes you along Oneida Lake, you'll miss too much of the grand old Erie.

Two distinct canals were built to link the Erie Canal with Oneida Lake. The first Oneida Lake Canal left the Erie

Cyclists meet a mule-drawn canal boat on the old Erie Canal.

at Higginsville and entered Oneida Lake at the mouth of the Wood Creek. A careful search will reveal the old canal bed, but little else. An improved Oneida Lake Canal was built further west. I haven't found any remains, but they are out there, somewhere.

Visiting the Oneida Indian Nation

The Oneida Indian Nation, one of the first five Haudenosaunee nations, played a critical part in the success of the American Revolution. You will have learned about this if you bicycled by the Herkimer home near Little Falls, through the Oriskany Battlefield, or by Fort Stanwix in Rome. To find out more, take a short side trip to the Oneida cultural center located on NY 46 five

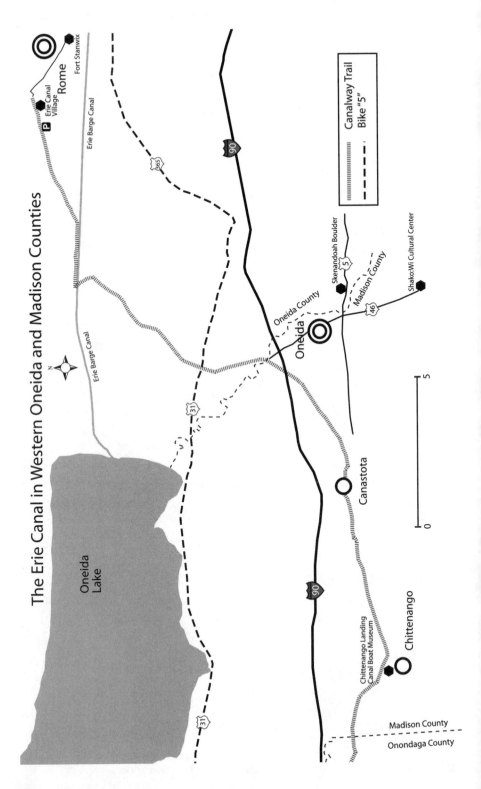

The Erie Canal in Western Oneida and Madison Counties

Oneida Lake

Fort Stanwix

Rome

Erie Canal Village

P

Erie Barge Canal

365

90

N

Erie Barge Canal

31

Oneida County

Skenandoah Boulder

5

Madison County

Oneida

46

Shako:Wi Cultural Center

Canastota

31

90

Chittenango Landing
Canal Boat Museum

Chittenango

Madison County

Onondaga County

Canalway Trail

Bike "5"

0   5

and one-half miles south of the Old Erie Canal Historic State Park towpath.

To get to the Shako:Wi Cultural Center, get on to NY 46 where it turns and crosses over the old canal near Durhamville and head into the city of Oneida. Follow it through Oneida past the intersection with NY 5, and ride another two miles south on NY 46. You'll arrive at the center where you can learn about the Haudenosaunee and the critically indispensable role the Oneida's played in the Revolution. Check out the arts and crafts on display.

After visiting the center, return to the Canalway Trail as you came, following NY 46 back to the Old Erie Canal State Park.

However there is one more interesting very short detour, a visit to the Skenandoah Boulder.

To visit the stone, head east on NY 5 exactly 1.2 miles from the intersection with NY 46. As you pass through village of Oneida Castle, on NY 5, note that this was once the site of the principal Oneida village, known as Kanonwalohale. After visiting the Skenandoah Boulder, return to NY 46 on NY 5, head north on NY 46 through Oneida to the Old Erie Canal State Park.

Back on the state park trail heading west, there are some interesting stopping points. In Canastota, you'll find a small canal museum. South of Canastota, five miles south on Oxford Road, at Nichols Pond Park, is the site of an Oneida Indian village attacked by Samuel de Champlain in 1615.

The Skenandoah Boulder is perhaps the largest syenite erratic.

Just How Do Canals Really Work?

A canal is a remarkably energy-efficient system and it's all powered by gravity. First, the summit level has to be supplied with enough water to feed virtually the entire canal. The Erie Canal had three summit levels, two here in Central New York. Water that flowed into Central New York's long level flowed both north down the Oswego Canal to Lake Ontario and east all the way down the Mohawk Valley to the Hudson River. Many reservoirs and feeder canals kept the summit levels full of water throughout the rainy and dry seasons. All canals leak some so additional feeders were used to keep the lower stretches of canal supplemented with additional water as needed.

Going down? Boats going both down and/or up the canal descended and/or ascended in small steps or increments through stone locks. A descending boat simply entered a lock at its upper/higher end; the upper wooden gate was opened while the lower wooden gate was kept closed. Once inside, the upper gate was closed by hand; small valves in the lower gate were then opened by hand, permitting the water to flow out until the water level of the lower end was reached. Now, water pressure helped form a tight seal at the upper gate, which became, in effect, a dam holding back the higher water level. But as the lower gate was now equalized with the lower water level, a mere push by hand permitted it to open. The boat was towed out. Water seeks its own level so the descending boat merely went along for the ride. No pumps were used. It all happened because of gravity and hand-power.

Going up? Again, it is merely gravity at work, assisted by hand-power at the lock gates. A boat going up enters the lock with its lower gate opened to the lower water level. The upper gate is a small wooden dam holding back the waters of the upper canal level. Once inside the stone lock, the lower gates are closed by hand. The locktender then walked to the upper end of the lock, opened small valves in the upper gate and water slowly filled the lock, flowing downhill, but raising the water level in the lock chamber. With the gates closed, the boat ascends with the rising water in the lock. Once the water level in the lock is equalized with the upper water level, gravity stops the water flow. The lower wooden gate has become the small dam holding back the canal waters. The upper gate is swung open by hand and the boat towed out.

O neida" ("Onyota'a:ka) means "people of the standing stone." Oneida legend says that the Oneida were led to these lands by following a moving stone; where it stopped, they settled. There is another ice-age linkage here because glaciers move staggering amounts of loose stone and boulders (glaciers are made up of about one-third stone and two-thirds ice) and deposit these stones as erratics. Erratics are non-native stones and boulders which can be found all over New York. Syenite is one type of erratic and is frequently found in Oneida territories The Skenandoah Boulder is perhaps the largest syenite erratic. It is named for a very famous Oneida Chief Skenandoah, who was a close friend of Benjamin Franklin.

Following the old Erie Canal five miles further to the village of Chittenango, you'll find the restored, old canal dry docks at the Chittenango Landing Canal Boat Museum. This is a worthwhile stop where you can get a good picture of what the old Erie looked like. There is an interpretive center, the dry docks, and a sawmill-blacksmith complex. Also in Chittenango is the birthplace of L. Frank Baum, author of the *Wizard of Oz*. Chittenango has yellow brick sidewalks and an Oz Festival each May. Baum's birthplace is on NY 13, south of the village.

If you find the lack of pavement along the towpath to be troublesome, excellent low-volume local roads follow the old canal bed very closely. With a little road savvy you will have a very enjoyable trip and miss none of the important stops along the way. If you wander at all, you will come to the nearby tracks of the New York Central — built as the Utica & Syracuse Railroad.

A canal boat dry dock facility at Chittenango Landing Canal Boat Museum.

Madison County is one of my favorite spots to ride. It is quiet, rural, scenic, and loaded with interesting history. The distance from Fort Stanwix to the Oneida/Madison border is seventeen miles. The distance across Madison County on the state park route is about fifteen miles.

Chapter 12

Onondaga County

Onondaga County lies at the geographic center of the canal network; Sims Store is exactly halfway between Buffalo and Albany. The Erie Canal created the economic prosperity that helped build this part of New York State so there are many important canal sites. The Onondaga Nation of Haudenosaunee was always, and still is, keeper of the "central fire" of the Six Nations — this was their "capitol."

I f you are entering Onondaga County on Bike "5" you will be alongside the southern shore of Oneida Lake, the route of the Erie Barge Canal. You will then circle north around Syracuse.

If you are riding from the east on the Old Erie Canal Historic State Park towpath, you'll soon come upon the Poolsbrook Picnic Area, where there are restrooms and parking. Further ahead, just to the south of the canal, is the beautiful Green Lakes State Park complete with a bathing beach and camping areas. The Green Lakes are also significant glacial features. There are two lakes, two hundred feet deep, with a unique aquamarine color. Round Lake is a National Natural Landmark. It is a plunge pool, something like a giant pothole. If the potholes you saw on Moss Island were big enough for a few people to stand in, these two plunge pools are small lakes. They are formed in much the same way. Be sure to climb to the top of the park's access road, located above the golf course, to look down into and appreciate the beauty of the higher, unspoiled lake.

Continuing west from Green Lakes on the old towpath, just before crossing the Limestone Creek aqueduct, you'll see a small canal bed and towpath heading off to the south. This is a short stretch of old feeder canal that once connected the village of Fayetteville with the Erie Canal. If you have been traveling all the way from Rome and are looking for food or a place to stay before heading into Syracuse, you might try Fayetteville. The old feeder canal towpath will lead you right to the village center. This stretch of feeder canal is typical of many built to connect the old Erie Canal with small villages just off its course.

The Iroquois Confederation was governed from hilltops to the south of today's city of Syracuse. The Onondaga were the central tribe in the Iroquois Confederacy. A great longhouse still exists on a reservation south of Syracuse where the Council Fire is maintained. As we earlier learned, the Mohawk village of Ossernenon was the Eastern Door of the Confederacy. The Seneca settlement at Ganondogan was the Western Door. Here, on Onondaga lands was the location of the Council Fire of a symbolic Great Longhouse that extended for several hundred miles across what is now New York. This symbolism was important in uniting the five nations. With canoes and natural waterways, the Confederacy governed an Indian Empire extending about 150 miles to the east and west of this point. These Indians, collectively, called themselves the Haudenosaunee, or "People of the Longhouse." The French used the word "Iroquois." The British referred to these Indians as the Five Nations, and then Six Nations after the Tuscarora Nation was admitted to the confederacy.

The Old Erie Canal Park Trail ends at the Cedar Bay Picnic Area in Dewitt, a few miles west of Fayetteville and just outside the city of Syracuse.

In Syracuse, as in most upstate cities, the Erie Canal lies under modern highways. You have two cycling options for proceeding: return to Bike "5" or use busy, local city streets. I suggest that you get back to Bike "5" from the western end of Erie Canal State Park. Simply take any one of a number of quiet north-south local roads on the eastern side of Onondaga County that link the two; you will not get lost. I recommend Kirkville Road. Once back on Bike "5," follow it as it circles around the north side of Syracuse until it rejoins the Canalway Trail near Jordan. Sections of it are busy, but it is the best cycling choice.

Louis Rossi

Butternut Creek Aqueduct, east of Syracuse. The towpath now carries the Canalway Trail.

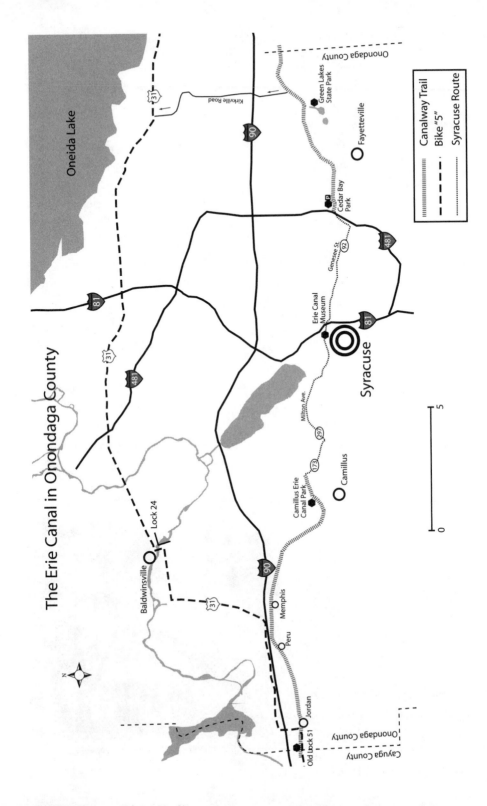

The Erie Canal in Onondaga County

Oneida Lake

Green Lakes
State Park

Onondaga County

Kirkville Road

Fayetteville

Cedar Bay
Park

Genesee St.

Erie Canal
Museum

Syracuse

Milton Ave.

Camillus Erie
Canal Park

Camillus

Lock 24

Baldwinsville

Memphis

Peru

Jordan

Old Lock 51

Onondaga County
Cayuga County

Canalway Trail
Bike "5"
Syracuse Route

If you choose to follow Bike "5," it is thirty-three miles all the way across Onondaga County. In Onondaga County, Bike "5" more closely follows the route of the Barge Canal. At Belgium and Baldwinsville, you will again cross over the

Travel Tip

Consider using the local bus service, CENTRO, to move you and your bike from the Canalway trailheads in DeWitt or Camillus to the Erie Canal Museum downtown. See the Resource Guide for more information.

Erie Barge Canal. There is a small canal park at Lock 24 in Baldwinsville.

Visiting Syracuse

In downtown Syracuse, you'll find the Erie Canal located in an old weighlock building, built in 1850. This is the only surviving weighlock out of the original seven. A weighlock is exactly what it seems — a place where canal boats are weighed and tolls collected. Tolls collected from the Erie Canal once paid the entire budget of the State of New York. An especially fascinating aspect of this building is the means of weighing the canal boats. Originally, when first opened, the simplest of all means was used. As the boat entered the lock, locktenders measured the volume of water it displaced. As the weight of water is a known constant (62.4 pounds per cubic foot), the amount of water displaced gave the weight of the boat through simple multiplication. The ancient Greeks knew this — it is called Archimedes Principle. Well, no self-respecting canal boat captain of the 1830s was going to believe any of that. Having just as much confidence in the government tax collector as we

Rich Simberg

The Weighlock Building in Syracuse holds the Erie Canal Museum.

Central New York Feeders

The Long Level from Utica to Syracuse was one of the summit levels of the Erie at an elevation of 429 feet. Water descended from this level in both directions; hence, the "summit" designation. Eastward, water flowed down through forty-six locks all the way to Albany. Water did not flow as far westward, as there was another short step-up on the Erie through Camillus, but northward, water flowed out of the Erie from downtown Syracuse down the Oswego canal, over 18 locks, into Lake Ontario. So it was critically important that enough water was supplied to the summit level to keep it full throughout the open season from spring to fall, regardless of rainfall levels. The canal builders were highly successful at this, building reservoirs near and far, and constructing a dozen canal feeders.

Exploring any of these feeders by bicycle requires nothing more than a good local road map. All the local roads are fine for on-road cycling and there are dozens of pleasant small towns and local parks. For example, to follow the Chittenango Creek Feeder, just head south from the Erie Canal at Chittenango on NY 13, which is a fine road for cycling. You'll do some climbing, going up through Chittenango Falls State Park and on to Cazenovia (nine miles total). Or, to trace the Skaneateles Lake Feeder, from Jordan on the Erie Canal, take any local road to the attractive village of Skaneateles, nine miles away.

do today, boaters insisted, and got, replacement of the original system with a complete system of cradles and scales. Until tolls were removed, boats would be weighed by draining the weighblock, allowing the boats to settle dry onto cradles, using "official weights" on scale beams.

Visiting the Canal Museum is worthwhile and will give you an excellent perspective on how the old Erie Canal shaped a major American city, which was built astride it. It has an excellent bookstore for canal buffs. It lies between Water Street and Erie Boulevard, behind City Hall. Erie Boulevard is a busy roadway built on top of the original canal bed. Therefore, getting to the Weighblock Building by bicycle is best left to off-peak travel periods. Since the old Erie Canal Towpath ends east of the city (in Dewitt) and resumes west of the city (in Camillus), and Bike "5" is circling north of the city on NY Route 31, an adventurous cyclist must make his or her way downtown over busy Syracuse streets. No route is really attractive. The route I recommend for a hardy cyclist on a direct cross-state-tour is as follows: From the end of the Canal Park in Dewitt, take Butternut Drive to Genesee Street (Route 5 and

92) and follow Genesee Street (NY Route 92) six miles from Dewitt to down-town. Traveling from west to east, it is difficult to make the left from Genesee onto Butternut (look for Pickwick) — the street is hard to find, the left turn is hazardous, and it is located in a busy interchange. This route is not easy, but it's the best option. Ride carefully.

Once in Syracuse, you'll find it has a very attractive downtown. Just a few blocks west of the Canal Museum (Weighlock Building) is Clinton Square. This was once the "harbor" of Syracuse, and the junction of the Erie and Oswego canals. Pictures in the Canal Museum will show you what this site once looked like. Of course, no one can replicate what it must have smelled like. In its heyday, jammed with horses and mules, with the canal itself serving as the toilet for canal boat passengers and crew, one can only imagine. Syracuse has plans to return this space to pedestrian use; it will be a beautiful spot when it does. There is a lot of interesting architecture awaiting you in Syracuse. Like all cities, its streets are busy during weekdays but much better for touring by bicycle on the weekend.

The Oswego Barge Canal diverges from the Erie Barge Canal north of Syracuse. The old Oswego Canal once began right in downtown Syracuse, at Clinton Square, near the Weighlock Building, and like all the canals of that time, was entirely separate from the natural riverbeds. See the next chapter for more details on the Oswego Canal.

After visiting the Erie Canal Museum and downtown Syracuse, follow Erie Boulevard westward (you are on top of the old canal) from downtown. At the intersection with West Genesee Street, turn westward; almost immediately, turn right onto Milton Avenue. As you leave Syracuse, you'll enter the town of Geddes. The town is named after James Geddes, who, more than anyone, is responsible for selecting the route of the Erie Canal across western New York. You will learn more about his work in Monroe County. Along this route, you will come alongside the old Auburn & Syracuse Railroad, another rail link in the first chain of railroads that crossed New York. NY 297 will join Milton Avenue; continue straight. You will enter the town of Camillus. At the intersection of NY 173, turn right. In one and one-half miles, the Erie Canalway trailhead will be on your left. Look for a small sign "Town of Camillus Erie Canal Park." If you come to Reed Webster Park, you've gone too far.

At Camillus, you are back on the original Erie Canal towpath. This section of path extends from Camillus across Onondaga and Cayuga counties.

Sims Store Museum in Camillus is a replica of an Erie Canal store.

However, unlike the section of towpath on the eastern side of Syracuse, which is a park under state jurisdiction, this stretch, the Camillus Erie Canal Park, is a local park maintained by volunteers. The volunteer work underway west of Syracuse in Onondaga County is impressive. You'll find many excellent interpretive signs to help explain canal history at this site. It is easy to visualize canal boats plying this section of Erie Canal. Perhaps no section of the old canal has been better restored than that in Camillus. Hundreds of volunteers cleared the canal bed, built dams, and filled the canal with water. A major improvement by the New York Canal Corporation was completed in 2006 to further improve the eleven-mile stretch from Camillus to Jordan. Canal boat tours run on Sundays from May to October.

After a short ride west, you will come to Sims Store Museum, the replica of a general store and departure station for persons riding canal boats. The original store was also a residence of John Sims and family. Local lore has it that baby Susie's carriage rolled into the canal with Susie aboard, perhaps persuading John to move his family elsewhere. Today, there are many Sims descendants in the Camillus area.

Be sure to ask questions at Sims Store. There is a lot of "hidden history" here for the true canal explorer which will be pointed out to you. Plans are to fully restore the 144-foot, 4-arch "Nine Mile Creek Aqueduct" which is just east of Sims Store. Once completed, this will be the only restored aqueduct of the original thirty-two on the Erie.

Heading west, conditions on the towpath have improved with the new federal renovation project. If the limestone trail is too wet, excellent paved local roads parallel the canal in this area and it is not difficult to follow the old canal by road. The old towpath goes through Warners, Memphis and Peru, all small canal communities. There is an interesting aqueduct and waste weir at Peru. Then it is on to Jordan, which is the first large town heading west. This is a good place to "refuel." In Jordan there is an interesting Erie Canal Park based around the "Jordan Aqueduct." Here you can walk through and under the aqueduct and admire the stonework that the craftsmen could build so well.

Louis Rossi

Excellent signage leaving Jordan. The Canalway Trail is on your left while Bike "5" continues westward.

You'll rejoin Bike "5" in Jordan, at the western edge of Onondaga County. Just west of Jordan, almost at the county line stands a small canal park built at Lock 51. This is directly adjacent (north side) to Bike "5," NY 31. Straight ahead is Cayuga County and more wonderful cycling along the historic Erie Canal.

Chapter 13

The Oswego Canal

*This ride takes you thirty-five miles through an area rich in
the history of the Revolutionary War, War of 1812, and early
European settlements. There is a lot to see along the Oswego Canal.
It is a multi-day side-trip well worth taking.
You'll have to be comfortable with on-road cycling, but the roads
are generally bike-friendly. You can get the local information you
need at the canalside centers at Phoenix, Fulton, and Oswego and
find small parks at every lock. Take a bit of care, stop and ask
for advice, and you'll have a great time.*

Fort Ontario

The Oswego Canal is very important in the history of New York State
canals. As an extension of the original Erie Canal to Lake Ontario, this
was one of the first feeder canals to be built. Construction of the first Oswego
Canal began on July 4, 1826, which marked the 50th anniversary of the
Declaration of Independence. This was exactly nine years after construction
began on the Erie Canal.

Like all the canals of that century, it was built entirely separate from the
wild rivers of New York. It stretched thirty-eight miles from the Erie Canal in
downtown Syracuse (adjacent to Clinton Square and the Weighlock Building)
northwards to Oswego. Eighteen locks were required to descend to Lake
Ontario from the 400-foot elevation of the Erie Canal in Syracuse. It took just
two years to complete the first Oswego Canal. The original canal went north
from the vicinity of the Weighlock Building, and followed the eastern shore
of Onondaga Lake to its outflow into the Seneca River. There it turned and
followed the banks of the Seneca River to Three Rivers, crossed the Oneida
River, and followed the eastern shore of the Oswego River all the way to
Lake Ontario.

Because this was such a busy canal, a new Oswego "Barge" Canal was built early in the 20th century. The present Oswego Canal is entirely in the Oswego River and stretches just twenty-four miles from the Erie Barge Canal at Three Rivers to

Travel Tip

CENTRO buses between Syracuse and Oswego will accept bicycles as baggage and there is service along the entire route. See the Resource Guide for more information.

Oswego. As the old Oswego Canal was converted to the Oswego River, the river water level was raised submerging canal features such as locks, canal walls, and much of the towpath. You can still spot a few of these historic remains. There are seven operating locks (Numbered 1 through 8; there is no number 4) required to descend 118 feet. Just like the locks on the Erie Barge Canal, each Oswego Canal lock is a small park. These attractive parks make good start/stop points for day trips, and the locktenders are a terrific source of local information and color.

Although there is no off-road route along the Oswego Canal, there are good on-road routes that will take you to historic sites of the old canal and trace the scenic route of today's canal. It is a ride well worth taking.

This cycling route is a work-in-progress, but a fascinating short side trip featuring live, operating canal history, some fine, small communities, as well as some important history. There is, as of yet, no uniformly-signed bike route and there are few completed off-road trail segments. Both counties and

Mud Lock is the best preserved of all the old Oswego Canal locks.

Louis Rossi

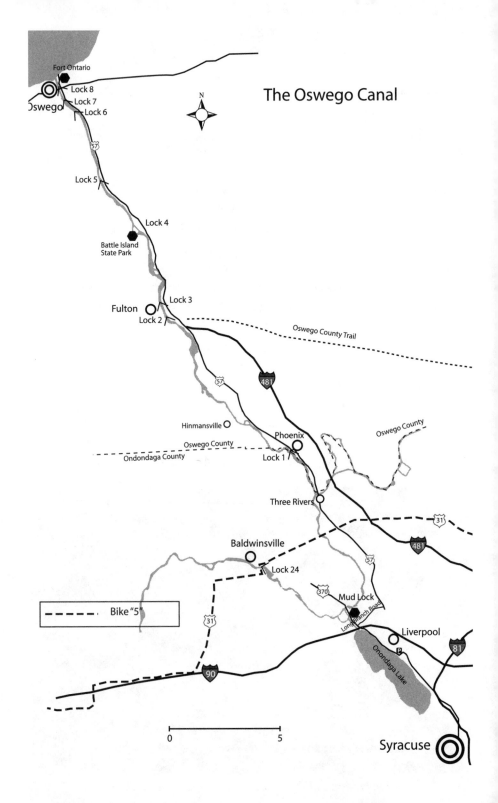

The Oswego Canal

Fort Ontario

Lock 8
Lock 7
Lock 6

Oswego

57

Lock 5

Lock 4

Battle Island
State Park

Lock 3

Fulton
Lock 2

Oswego County Trail

57

481

Hinmansville

Phoenix

Oswego County

Oswego County
Ondondaga County

Lock 1

Three Rivers

31

481

Baldwinsville

57

Lock 24

370

Mud Lock

Bike "5"

31

Long Branch Road

Liverpool

81

Onondaga Lake

90

0   5

Syracuse

bicycle advocates are working to put a bike route in place. Fortunately, there are many safe on-road choices, but they are not easily identified. Hopefully, at some time in the future, a numbered on-street bike route will be created, like Bike Routes "5" and "9," which will guide you safely and directly. You'll find this to be a pretty flat tour. Geologically, you are cycling down into the now dry lakebed of ancient Lake Iroquois, which as you've discovered earlier, is very important in making the Erie Canal possible.

Onondaga County: Syracuse to Three Rivers

The original Oswego Canal alignment went north, beginning just west of the Weighlock Building, along the west side of North Salina Street. There are some old canal ruins along this stretch, but it is a busy industrial area and not worth exploring. Follow North Salina Street, Park Street, and Old Liverpool Road into Onondaga Lake County Park. Alternatively, you might want to base yourself at the park and pick up the bike trail from there.

Enter Onondaga Lake Park and follow the trail along the east shore of Onondaga Lake. This popular recreation path is on top of the old Oswego Canal bed. There are some segments of separated bike path within the park and work is underway to complete a loop entirely circling Onondaga Lake.

Syracuse is known as the Salt City. The Salt Museum, located on the shore of Onondaga Lake in the park, was constructed from timbers taken from actual salt warehouses. There are barrels, kettles, and other equipment that were used to turn brine (salt water) into salt for the nation.

The first important canal site to see is Mud Lock, which is at the very northeastern-most point in Onondaga Lake Park, where the outflow of Onondaga Lake joins the Seneca River. Mud Lock, which gets its name from the unstable soil on which it was constructed, was built of wood in 1828. The present lock, incorporating features from 1862 and 1887 canal enlargements, was renovated during the Depression. Unlike most old locks, where only stonework remains, Mud Lock has significant portions of wooden lock gates and gate hardware. This makes it easier to understand the ingenuity of canal builders and makes this particular lock especially historic. Mud Lock is adjacent to the Seneca River which is now the route of the Erie Barge Canal.

From Mud Lock, you will have to bike on local roads north through Three Rivers. Take Long Branch Road to CR 57 (Oswego Road). You will cross NY 31 (Bike "5"). CR 57 can be a busy roadway so ride carefully. It is roughly six miles from downtown Syracuse to Mud Lock and another eight miles to Three Rivers.

Oswego County: Oneida River to Phoenix

At Three Rivers, you will enter Oswego County. Here, the historic Oneida Outlet Canal connected the original Oswego Canal through Oneida Lake to the old Erie Canal near Oneida. Today, the Oneida River is the route of the Erie Barge Canal. Cross over the Oneida River (Erie Barge Canal) and continue north to Phoenix following the Oswego River Road. Phoenix is the site of Lock 1 on the Oswego Barge Canal. Phoenix, like the other small towns and cities along the Oswego, is working to redevelop its canal heritage. Lock 1 offers some history to see, a nice park site, a bascule lift bridge, and the largest of the dams along the entire Oswego River. It is about two and one-half miles from Three Rivers to Phoenix.

Louis Rossi

Oswego County: Phoenix to Fulton

The Phoenix to Fulton segment is about eight and one-half miles. As noted earlier, the canalization of the Oswego River, about ninety years ago, resulted in flooding or removal of many old Oswego Canal sites. The remains of the Hinmansville Lock lie just north of the Hinmansville bridge on the east side of the Canal. There is another old lock on the east side just north of Ox Creek.

Pleasure boats using Lock 1 in Phoenix.

Fulton is the site of Barge Canal Locks 2 and 3. With its new canal harbor and visitor's center, attractive parks, and a variety of restaurants, it's a great stopping place. Fulton is the home of Nestle's and hosts a Chocolate Festival each summer.

Also near Fulton, just west of the city limits, you can find the Oswego County Trail. This is a rough and unpaved path that extends twenty-five miles eastward across Oswego County, from Fulton, to Cleveland on Oneida Lake. This trail, lying on the abandoned roadbed of the New York Ontario & Western Railway, is very rough and for off-road bicycles only.

Oswego County: Fulton to Oswego

It is about eleven miles from the city of Fulton directly north to the city of Oswego. Again, the only options are on-street cycle routes, but there are reasonably quiet roads to follow.

Continuing north, you pass Pathfinder Island, named after the title character in James Fenimore Cooper's *The Pathfinder,* on the east side of the channel. Much of the action in *The Pathfinder* takes place during a trip down the Oswego River in 1759 and the book describes a fictitious skirmish occurring on this island between the main character in the book, Natty Bumppo, and Huron Indians. Published in 1840, the book was written after Cooper served as a naval officer at Fort Ontario from 1808 to 1809.

Battle Island State Park is named for a July 3, 1756 skirmish nearby between the French and their Indian allies and the British. British soldiers who were traveling by boat to Albany were attacked and fought from the small island. Fighting from the island was advantageous since trees helped to shelter and conceal the soldiers. The British were also better armed than their enemies, and the French retreated after about an hour. The islands have changed due to cannel construction and erosion, but Battle Island State Park marks the general location.

<small>Oswego County Department of Promotion & Tourism</small>

The O&W rail trail tunnel at Oswego is unique in all New York. It connects the Oswego River with Fort Ontario.

As you cycle north, you won't find a Barge Canal Lock 4 but Lock 5 is in Minetto along the west shore of the River.

Locks 6, 7 and 8 are in Oswego. In Oswego, a short section of old rail bed has been paved and opened for cycling. This includes a unique tunnel section. There is nothing else like it anywhere else along New York State's canals.

The rail trail leads directly to Fort Ontario, an extraordinarily well-preserved stone fort dating from 1755. This fort was specifically provided for in the Treaty of Paris, which settled Revolutionary War disputes, because it was so important to the defense of the new Republic.

Fort Ontario is the third fort constructed in the area by the British. Earlier, they had built Forts Oswego and George on the west shore of the river to protect their fur trade from the French. The French later destroyed both forts. Fort Ontario was destroyed during the French and Indian War in 1756 and rebuilt by the British in 1759. It was then burned by the British during the War of 1812 and repaired in the 1830s. Fort Ontario was used again during World War II, when it provided safety for refugees fleeing Nazi persecution in Europe. It was the only site in the United States to accept refugees at that time.

As you head toward the lake, you'll come to the H. Lee White Marine Museum which depicts three centuries of nautical history of the Oswego Harbor and Lake Ontario. Many artifacts and hands-on exhibits are displayed. You'll find the museum's canal exhibit on Derrick Boat #8, moored on the west side of the West First Street pier. Built in 1925 and used for lock repair and canal dredging, the Derrick Boat is the last remaining steamboat on the New York State Canal.

The Port of Oswego is the first U.S. port of call on the Great Lakes from the St. Lawrence Seaway, so you may well see an ocean-going vessel unloading or a sleek sailing ship from the Midwest. With all the canal refurbishments and sights to see, Oswego makes an excellent overnight rest stop.

The Oswego Canal tour can be an out-and-back loop ride from the Erie Canal in Syracuse. However, you need not double-back to Syracuse. There are many, many other touring opportunities that open-up from Oswego.

Travel Tip

At Minetto (between Fulton and Oswego) one of Adventure Cycling's transcontinental bike routes crosses the route of the Oswego Canal. See the Resource Guide for more information.

Other Touring Options

The famous 450-plus mile Seaway Trail stretches all along New York State's northern border — along the Saint Lawrence River, Lake Ontario, the Niagara River and Lake Erie. If you head northeast from Oswego, the Seaway Trail will take you to the great Eisenhower Locks at Massena. The Seaway Trail is perhaps the best organized, most professionally-run of all the state's scenic byways.

One multi-day trip eastward over to the Black River Canal (Chapter 10) is also practical because there are so many good local roads and state highways connecting Oswego with Carthage or Lowville. Both Carthage and Lowville are about seventy-five miles from Oswego. Heading south to Oneida, you can then pick up the Erie Canal back to Syracuse. The total mileage of this loop is two hundred miles or more.

The previously mentioned Oswego County Trail extends twenty-six miles east from near Maple Avenue in Fulton to the Village of Cleveland on Oneida Lake. It makes a connection to the Erie Canal near Oneida or Rome (roughly fifty miles) very practical. If you find the trail conditions unacceptable, you'll also find quiet local roads alongside.

A shorter loop option is to head west from Oswego toward Cayuga County, where there are several off-road trail options. It is about fifteen miles, on-road, west along NY 104, the Seaway Trail, to Fair Haven State Park. This is a beautiful lakeshore park with interesting ice-age geological features. Fair Haven is the northern end of the Cayuga County Trail, which extends twelve miles south to Cato, where you are just eight miles, on-road, from the Erie Canal at Weedsport. If you find biking conditions on the Cayuga County Trail unsuitable, there are good on-road biking options paralleling the route. You can then bike the Erie Canal trails back to a starting point near Syracuse.

The on-road bicycling opportunities involving a tour of the Oswego Canal are numerous. We've suggested some options — there are others. Contact the Oswego County tourism office for current road information and lodging ideas. Reach out to local bicycling clubs for suggested itineraries. Remember to consider using the CENTRO bus service. Put yourself in an exploratory mood and have fun!

Chapter 14

Cayuga and Seneca Counties

You have two options heading west out of Jordan: The Erie Canalway Trail (local signs say "Cayuga County Trail"), which extends all the way across Cayuga County, or Bike "5," which is almost directly adjacent to the old canal and offers a continuous, safe on-road alternative. The modern Erie Barge Canal runs parallel about three miles to the north. It's about thirteen miles across this short section, but there is a lot to see. This is flat, easy cycling and you'll be visiting several "ports of call" starting with Weedsport, then Centerport, and finally Port Byron, all within a distance of five miles.

You might consider a diversion from Weedsport to the city of Auburn. Just eight miles south on NY 34, Auburn is packed with historical heritage. There's the home of William Seward, President Lincoln's Secretary of State, and the person responsible for the purchase of Alaska. Close by, there's the home of Harriet Tubman, who was closely associated with abolition and the Underground Railway.

At Centerport, be sure to see the Centerport Aqueduct Historic Site. It is on the Cayuga County Trail and directly adjacent to Bike "5" on the south side.

While the Cayuga County Trail might be a bit hard to follow and conditions a little too difficult for narrow, high-pressure tires, it is worth trying. If conditions are too rough, it is easy to follow the towpath by adjacent paved road. Remember, Bike "5" is always alongside to redirect you safely back on course.

Cayuga County is trying very hard to be bicycle-friendly. Plan on spending some time here. For the off-road cyclist there are many trails to explore — not just old canals, but rail trails as well. And most local roads are quiet and cycle-friendly. Be prepared to explore a little. A trick is to look for street names like Dock Street, Lock Street, Towpath Road, Water Street, Erie Street or Erie Boulevard, and so forth. These are often access points to old canal sites.

hat were land-locked "ports" doing in Central New York? As construction of the canal progressed west of Syracuse, new territory was being opened. No longer was the "modern" canal transportation linking up old villages. Now, for the first time, new places were springing up along the expanding canal. These promising sites were major "ports" in their day.

A test for the skillful canal explorer is to try to find the ruins of the Seneca River Aqueduct. This aqueduct was 840 feet long with 31 stone arches. Hint: It is near the village of Montezuma.

The Cayuga County website contains downloadable trail maps and other useful information for the biker-tourist.

As there are so many canal options in this area, you might consider establishing a base in one of Cayuga County's attractive small canal towns. Based there, you can bike east as far as you wish toward Syracuse one day, west to Seneca Falls the next, north to Lake Ontario the third, and on into Wayne County the next. A trip south to the vineyards of the Finger Lakes is possible as well. You will find local roads in this area excellent for cycling, so both on and off-road rides are feasible.

North of Weedsport, at Cato, a fifteen-mile rail trail extends north to Lake Ontario at Fair Haven. It is an eight-mile ride on NY 34, another excellent state highway, from Weedsport to Cato. Cycling

The Centerport Aqueduct Historic Site is an excellent example of Erie Canal stonework.

on NY 34 will bring you face to face to the extensive field of drumlins (whale-shaped hills formed by glacial action) that extends across the Lake Ontario plain. At Cato, turn left onto NY 370 and you will come to the unpaved rail trail in a very short distance. The rail trail extends north to Lake Ontario at Fair Haven, site of an excellent state park. As Fair Haven is fifteen miles west of Oswego, a loop is quite practical. (See previous chapter on the Oswego Canal.) The rail trail enters Fair Haven on Main Street where you'll find a small sign "Cayuga County Trail" directing you to Cato. It is just two-tenths of a mile

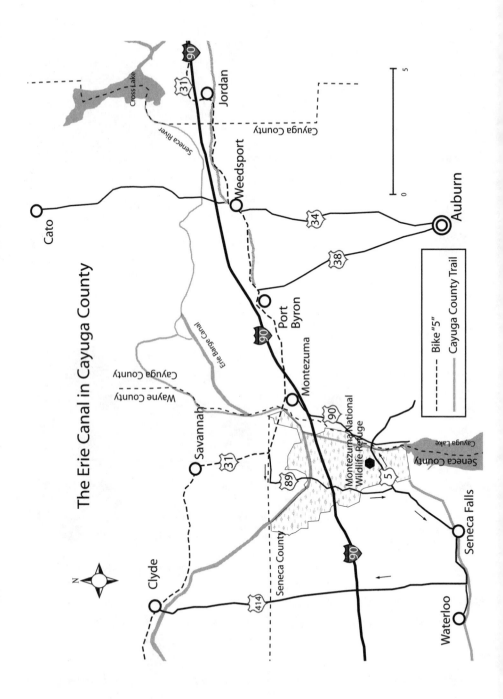

The Erie Canal in Cayuga County

to Fair Haven Beach State Park where you'll see unique sculpted bluffs — the result of erosion of drumlins by Lake Ontario's wave action. This rail trail, which sits on top of an old Lehigh Valley rail bed, is not always in the best condition. The Lehigh Valley used this line to reach its coal docks on Lake Ontario to export anthracite coal to Canada.

The Cayuga County Trail is great for mountain and hybrid bikes.

Before you leave Cayuga County and enter Seneca County, you also have the option of visiting the nearby Montezuma National Wildlife Refuge. This is an enormous swamp — another glacial feature. Think of it as an enormous plugged-up Finger Lake filled with almost bottomless muck. Creating a "waterproof" Erie Canal (that is, a canal bed that would hold canal water and not let it all seep out into the swamps) across this topography was another engineering challenge for canal builders. These same swamplands today are a major bird sanctuary.

The visitors center is located south of Bike "5," on NY 5 & 20. A slight detour will take you there. Look for the left turn on NY 89 and take it southbound. Right after you cross the barge canal (you can visit Lock 26), you'll see Tschache Pool up ahead. The flooded timber area of Tschache Pool

Erosion by ice is just one of the powerful forces of glaciation. The other is deposition, which is the movement and transfer of soils and rocks. A drumlin is a very visible result of deposition and there are about 10,000 drumlins in the Onondaga-Cayuga-Seneca-Wayne area. This, too, is geologically extraordinary. Drumlins are small egg-shaped hills oriented in a north-to-south direction. They are typically about 200 feet tall and can be anywhere from 400 feet to a mile in length. The north face of the hill is always the steep slope. Drumlins are composed of fine soils deposited by running streams at the edge of a glacier. You'll see many as you cycle through Cayuga and Wayne counties.

is a heron rookery. Take a moment and look over the pool. Note the nests in the stark, dead trees in the distance. Some of these are bald eagle sites. In 1976, the refuge and the NYS Department of Environmental Conservation began to release

Stopping at the Montezuma National Wildlife Refuge.

eagles at Montezuma. Through 1980, twenty-three eagles were released. Bald eagles have returned to Montezuma and have reared young. You can continue south on NY 89 and visit other unique sites in the wildlife refuge. The US Fish & Wildlife Service administers the 7,000-acre refuge. There is an information center located on Route 5 & 20 which is staffed in the summer and which has restrooms and an observation platform. The service does not permit bikes on refuge roads and trails; do not ride there without permission.

To continue to follow the Erie Canal westward toward Buffalo, you'll need to be on Bike "5." Follow it across the Seneca River into Seneca County. It's a short ride across a portion of the Montezuma Swamp and, in less than one mile, you'll arrive at the border of Wayne County. This whole section is only thirty-three flat miles on Bike "5" which generally is a very good road with just a few busy and congested stretches. Following the canal trails is slower but safer and more direct.

The Cayuga-Seneca Canal connects to the Erie Canal near the village of Montezuma. It travels south, through the Montezuma National Wildlife Refuge, then southwest in an artificial channel through Seneca Falls, Waterloo, and Geneva. For cyclists, the Cayuga-Seneca provides an important opportunity to reach the Finger Lakes "Wine Country" of New York. Along the route, in Seneca Falls, is the hub of America's women's suffrage movement. And there are excellent on-road routes that will take you around the eleven Finger Lakes and to the Pennsylvania border. The next chapter will describe this fascinating little canal and invite you to tour the beautiful Finger Lakes region.

Chapter 15

The Cayuga-Seneca Canal and Finger Lake Feeder Canals

The Cayuga-Seneca Canal and the feeder canals of the Finger Lakes offer some wonderful cycling in a very scenic and history-steeped area of the state. Not only can you reach the Finger Lakes "Wine Country" and think that you are riding in Italy, you also can visit Seneca Falls, once the hub of America's women's suffrage movement. There are excellent on-road routes taking you around the eleven Finger Lakes and to the Pennsylvania border. Because the Cayuga-Seneca Canal links the northern ends of Cayuga and Seneca lakes to the Erie Canal, communities like Ithaca and Montour Falls have canal facilities that can be reached by boat from the Atlantic Ocean or the Great Lakes. This chapter will introduce you to many riding options and day trips.

M any people think of the Cayuga-Seneca Canal as just a very interesting twelve-mile canal linking a few attractive, historic lakeside communities to the Erie Canal. Wrong — it is very much more than that. From its beginnings about 180 years ago, canal builders included the giant Cayuga and Seneca lakes, each about forty miles long, in the Cayuga-Seneca Canal system. This extended its reach to Ithaca and Watkins Glen, at the southern tips of these two giant lakes. There, at places, additional canals were built. The Chemung Canal reached beyond Seneca Lake to the headwaters of the Chemung (Susquehanna) River and reached into Pennsylvania. Finally, a third Finger Lake, Keuka Lake, was connected. That's why there are ports, like Branchport, and Hammondsport, land-locked deep in the heart of New York State. Overall, at its peak, the canal network based on the Cayuga-Seneca Canal extended almost 200 miles. While the "Grand Erie" is recognized, world-wide, as a political and engineering triumph, the network of canals based on the Cayuga-Seneca, which extends throughout the beautiful Finger Lakes Region, is another very impressive accomplishment in the history of canals. This chapter is dedicated to the adventurous on-road bicycle-tourist who is seeking friendly roads, awesome scenery, picturesque villages, and canal history. It is in three parts. First, a detailed itinerary is provided for touring the Cayuga-Seneca Canal. The second part describes a tour of Cayuga Lake and the Cayuga Inlet Canal, and last is a tour of Seneca Lake and its historic feeder canals.

The Cayuga-Seneca Canal

At present, no specifically numbered on-road routes exist, but nearly all the roadways in this part of New York are excellent for cycling with wide shoulders and rolling hills. First, I'll guide you village-by-village from the junction of the Erie Canal near Montezuma, though Seneca Falls, Waterloo, and to Geneva. Then, for the adventurous long-distance bicyclist, I will describe some trips along the many feeder canals that once extended the reach of the Cayuga-Seneca Canal to Pennsylvania.

Louis Rossi

Lock 1 raises boats from the level of the Erie Canal to the 384-foot elevation of Cayuga Lake.

One of the old mill buildings in Seneca Falls that relied upon waterpower.

Montezuma to Seneca Falls

Basic on-road tour directions are pretty simple. If you have arrived in the Village of Montezuma on your Erie Canal tour, whether you have come from the east or west, or along Bike "5" (NY 31) or the Canalway Trail, head south on NY 90, a designated NY State Scenic Byway. In about four miles you'll come to the junction with Route 5 & 20. (Note: To find Cayuga-Seneca Barge Canal Lock 1, you need to take a short dead-end detour. Continue south on NY 90; do not turn at US 20. Lock 1 is about one mile south of the junction.)

To follow the canal to Seneca Falls, Waterloo, and Geneva, turn west on Route 5 & 20. This will take you by the Montezuma National Wildlife Refuge main entrance (as noted in the previous chapter, worth stopping at) and in a total of just five miles you'll arrive right in Seneca Falls. Plan on spending some time here.

The village of Seneca Falls takes its name from a now-vanished sixty-foot waterfall. The original canal required six locks, with lifts ranging from six to ten feet to overcome the waterfall on this site. When the canal was rebuilt, almost a century ago, two larger locks, Cayuga-Seneca Barge Canal Locks 2 and 3, replaced the older, smaller ones, and a large new lake, Van Cleef Lake, was created. Just off the canal, on Fall Street, is the Seneca Museum of Waterways and Industry. The museum has excellent dioramas explaining the complicated canal history here. Indeed, there are three canal alignments and, like the archeology of ancient Troy, they all lie atop one another.

The Cayuga-Seneca Canal

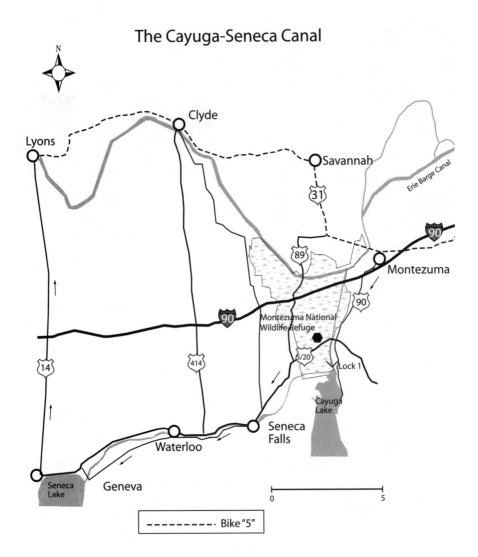

One of the many shops in Seneca Falls.

Right in the center of Seneca Falls are the National Women's Hall of Fame and the Women's Rights National Historic Park. In the mid-1840s the canals of New York were the nation's primary arteries of information as well as commerce. The modern thinking that flowed along the canal's waters had a lot to do with energizing the women's rights movement. Across the canal, nearby, is the 1847 home of Elizabeth Cady Stanton who was a driving force in the women's rights movement for fifty years. Anyone interested in women's history should spend a day in Seneca Falls.

Continuing west, you can ride on either US 20 (a busy road) or cross over the canal in Seneca Falls (on NY 414), turn west on to County Road 117 (CR 117), and ride four miles to the village of Waterloo. In Waterloo, CR 117 becomes CR119, which will take you to the end of the Cayuga-Seneca Canal

There is a close linkage between the National Women's Suffrage movement based in Central New York and Haudenosaunee sites. Only Haudenosaunee women could vote for tribal chiefs; men could not vote. The fact that this was going on so close by was an important impetus to the suffragettes. Not too far away are the chief sites of the historic Cayuga and Seneca tribes. The principal Cayuga home was located near the village of Union Springs, on NY 90, about five miles directly south of the junction between NY 90 and US 20. Not much remains here. A bit further west (described in the following chapter) lies the site of the prime Seneca village, Ganondagan. This is an important historic site open to the public.

on Seneca Lake in another four miles. I suggest following the quieter county roads, CR 117 and 119. Locally, these county roads are known as West Bayard Street, East River Street, and West River Street. Between Seneca Falls and Geneva, plans are underway to build a segment of Canalway Trail atop an old Lehigh Valley Railroad branch line that follows the south shore of the Cayuga-Seneca Canal. It should be completed in 2007.

Finally, in Waterloo is Cayuga-Seneca Barge Canal Lock 4, which completes the lift to the 441-foot level of Seneca Lake. The first canal had two locks (with a lift of about seven feet each) at this site. Look for Oak Island Park, just west of the center of town. Two canal alignments can be found here.

You will see an active rail branch line as you cycle, on or off-road, through Seneca Falls, Waterloo, and into Geneva. This was one of the original parts of the New York Central Railroad, first named the Auburn and Rochester Railroad, built in 1836. Soon afterward, a more direct railroad route was built, more closely following the Erie Canal through Newark and Lyons. But the railroad you see was one of the first in America.

The Cayuga-Seneca Canal is yet another of the original, early canals of New York that was converted into a "modernized" barge canal early in the last century. The original Cayuga-Seneca left the Erie Canal near Montezuma and extended to both Cayuga and Seneca lakes. It was completed in 1828. Eleven locks were required to create a navigable waterway between the Erie Canal and these two giant Finger Lakes.

The Cayuga-Seneca Canal ends at the northeast corner of Seneca Lake and the city of Geneva is located at the northwest corner. You can reach this picturesque city by cycling through Seneca Lake State Park or on-road. Geneva is an excellent base for cycle touring throughout the Finger Lakes. For those

The Cayuga-Seneca Canal had several feeder canals. At the south end of Cayuga Lake, at Ithaca, there was the short Cayuga Inlet Canal, opened in 1832. At Dresden, on Seneca Lake, the Crooked Lake Canal linked Keuka Lake, at Penn Yan, to the canal network. Keuka Lake is almost 250 feet higher than Seneca Lake, and twenty-eight locks were required to make this short eight-mile connection. Lastly, at the southern extremity of Seneca Lake, at Watkins Glen, the Chemung Canal was extended southward to Elmira and on to Pennsylvania. Although the Crooked Lake Canal and Chemung Canal were subsequently abandoned, the Cayuga-Seneca Barge Canal, and its feeder canals at Ithaca and Watkins Glen survive today. Today, four large locks link the Erie Canal and New York's two largest Finger Lakes.

A Note on Visiting the Finger Lakes

You've arrived in the region of New York's Finger Lakes. There are eleven glacial lakes, ranging in length from Cayuga, the longest at 40 miles, to Canadice, at just three miles. These are dramatic glacial features, geologically akin to the giant alpine lakes in Italy, and are a result of ice gouging by a polar icecap that extended over what is now upstate New York. The gouging created very deep lakes with depths well below sea level. Seneca Lake is the deepest with a depth of 632 feet while Cayuga is second deepest at 435 feet.

As you bicycle from north-to-south, you'll leave the flat plain that was ancient, glacial Lake Iroquois and head into the northern edge of the Appalachian Plateau. This is the north edge of the mountain chain that extends all the way to Georgia. This means hills, and sometimes big ones. The eleven Finger Lakes sit in valleys carved into the Appalachians during the last ice age. As you'll discover, canal builders used these passageways, as did the Cayuga and Seneca Indians before them, to achieve relatively flat transportation corridors. Today it makes great cycling, but expect serious and scenic climbs up major hills, if you diverge from the glacially-scoured lakebeds and rivers and explore the beautiful surrounding countryside.

For many reasons, including the stabilizing atmospheric effects caused by these giant lakes, this is also great wine country, making cycling here still more like cycling in Italy. There are well over fifty wineries open to the public. The region is also home to dozens of beautiful state parks. One, Taughannock Falls State Park on the southwestern shore of Cayuga Lake contains a 215-foot high waterfall, New York's tallest single drop. Another, Sampson State Park located mid-way down the eastern shore of Seneca Lake, was once a World War II Naval Base used to develop and test America's emerging submarine technology. With depths over 600 feet, Seneca Lake was an excellent and secure location to experiment in secrecy. Because of crush-depth limitations, WWII submarines couldn't dive much deeper than Seneca Lake. There is a Naval Memorial Museum located in the State Park.

Cycling in the Finger Lakes region is merely a matter of your cycling skill and stamina. There are almost no bad routes. Circumnavigating Cayuga or Seneca Lakes, or any of the eleven lakes, is entirely possible on the local roads. Expect hilly, if not mountainous terrain; this area is not flat, especially as you head south. There are dozens of attractive small towns to find lodging and food and countless public and private campsites. County tourism offices do a good job promoting bicycling and should be contacted directly. See the Resource Section for more information.

cyclists interested in exploring the several feeder canals that once connected to Seneca Lake, Geneva is a good launching point.

Here you have two choices. If you are heading back to the Erie Canal, take NY 14 or any of the roads heading north to the village of Lyons. If you wish to explore the many other canals that form a part of the Cayuga-Seneca Canal system, and are prepared for some long-distance diversions, read on.

Cayuga Lake and the Cayuga Inlet Canal

Cayuga Lake is the longest of the Finger Lakes. Back in the 1820s the Cayuga Inlet Canal was constructed at its southern end to provide a connection to Ithaca. This canal is still in service today and is a highly attractive tourist destination. If you have the stamina for a hard one-day Century-ride, or preferably a two-day scenic ride, follow my course below — I call it "Odyssey to Ulysses" for several reasons. Ancient Ithaca, back in Greece, was Ulysses' hometown. Adjacent to Ithaca, New York, is the town of Ulysses, which you will ride through. Homer's *Odyssey* described Ulysses' trip home from the destruction of Troy to Ithaca.

Odyssey to Ulysses Ride

From the northern tip of Cayuga Lake, follow NY 90 south. It is a very scenic road. You will pass many historic markers identifying Cayuga Indian sites and still more identifying battles of the Clinton-Sullivan campaign to destroy the Cayuga Nation. (You'll now also see many unofficial markers over Indian land disputes.) When you come to NY 34B, turn right, south. When you come to NY 34, turn right, south, toward Ithaca. NY 34 will take you into Ithaca; you'll find the Cayuga Inlet Canal on your right-hand side. You'll find food and lodging in Ithaca, a bicycle-friendly city. And you'll find a lighthouse, too.

The city of Ithaca, home to Cornell University and Ithaca College, is well known for its gorges. There are several spectacularly scenic gorges that are unique and have short walking trails through them, letting you get close to their many waterfalls and providing some impressive views. In the city try hiking up Fall Creek or Cascadilla gorges, which lead to the Cornell campus. Close by, outside Ithaca, the gorges are in state parks. Taughannock Falls Park to the north is on NY 89, and Buttermilk Falls Park and Enfield Falls (the latter is in Treman State Park) are both a short distance to the southwest of Ithaca off NY 13. Treman State Park has two entrances about two miles apart, one for its upper falls and one for its lower falls. You can bicycle between them on NY 327.

After touring the inlet canal, look for NY 89 and head north along the western shore of Cayuga Lake. You'll ride through the town of Ulysses, right past Taughannock Falls State Park (be sure to stop and see New York's highest waterfall). NY 89 will take you all the way back to the northern tip of Cayuga

Lighthouses on the Erie Canal

19th Century American ballads make references to "raging storms" on the Erie Canal. Well, you know by now that Clinton's Ditch was just four feet deep, was ultimately deepened to as much as nine feet, and avoided all the natural lakes and rivers of New York. There were no lighthouses on those canals. However, when the enlarged barge canals were built and the rivers and lakes were utilized, lighthouses were needed in a few places. The Erie Barge Canal has a lighthouse at each end of Oneida Lake (one at Verona State Park; the other at Brewerton). The lighthouse at Verona State Park is easily accessible from Bike "5," just a few miles north on NY 13. At Ithaca, at the Cayuga Inlet Canal, there are two lighthouses. In addition, a lighthouse fan will find lighthouses where the Oswego Canal enters Lake Ontario and the Erie Canal enters Lake Erie.

Ted Smith

A small lighthouse near the entrance to the Cayuga Inlet Canal.

Lake. I have identified the most direct route, but feel free to explore, as there are many attractive local roads for cycling.

Seneca Lake, Chemung Canal, and Crooked Lake Canal

Seneca Lake is the second longest Finger Lake and the deepest with a maximum depth of 618 feet. Since its surface elevation is 444 feet, that means its bottom is 174 feet below sea level. Glacial ice did that. Seneca Lake was always a part of the Cayuga-Seneca network of canals and today a short part of the historic Chemung Canal remains in service connecting Watkins Glen, at the lake's southern tip, to Montour Falls. It takes two or three days to see all this region has to offer. I will describe a lengthy loop ride that will take you around Seneca Lake, past all the feeder canals, alongside Keuka Lake, and through the town of Italy, where I'll describe the "Giro d'Italy, New York."

From the northern tip of Seneca Lake, you'll want to follow NY 96A (or divert to CR 125) south past Sampson State Park formerly an important naval depot. You might see on your left (east) the Seneca Army Depot. This was once one of America's largest nuclear weapon stockpiles. You can follow NY 96A through Ovid (a good food stop) or divert to CR 131. Then follow NY 414 which will take you directly into Watkins Glen and right to the old Chemug Canal (see text following). To return north, you'll want to follow NY 14. You can follow NY 14 all the way back to the northern tip of Seneca Lake. But about half-way there, at Dresden, you'll come upon the Crooked Lake Canal, a worthwile and interesting diversion described later on. And if you follow the Crooked Lake Canal to Penn Yan, you can ride the special "Giro D'Italy." Because of the many route options, your final road back to Geneva, at the northern tip of Seneca Lake, might not be NY 14.That's OK, as there are a lot of safe, scenic bike routes in this area.

Chemung Canal

The Chemung Canal, completed in 1833, connected Seneca Lake with the Chemung River and, ultimately, the Susquehanna River. The canal allowed the shipment of Pennsylvania anthracite coal, lumber, and agricultural products to the Erie Canal system, leading to the growth of Elmira as a regional center of manufacturing. The canal had a short life, rendered obsolete by the coming of the railroads in the late 1840s and 1850s.

Queen Catharine Montour, for whom the town of Catharine and village of Montour Falls were named, was a descendant of Madame Montour. Adopted by Frontenac, the French Governor of Canada, she married an Oneida Chief. In September 1779, as part of the campaign against the Iroquois, soldiers led by Sullivan and Clinton destroyed the Seneca village known as Catherine's Town. She escaped, but all buildings were burned.

The distance from the southern tip of Seneca Lake to the Pennsylvania border is only about twenty-five miles as the crow flies. In this short distance, Chemung Canal builders had to climb almost 500 feet. Forty-four locks climbed from the lake level to Horseheads. There the canal split. One leg went to the Chemung River at Elmira, descending five locks; the other went west, climbed four locks to reach the Chemung River at Gibson, near Corning. Here at Gibson, back in the 19th Century you were ninety-five miles by barge from the Erie Canal.

There is very little remaining of the canal system. Several miles remain open as part of the barge canal system between Watkins Glen and Montour Falls. You can follow it, on-road, on NY 14. Both communities are great stopping points. One of the main tourist attractions of Montour Falls is the 165-foot Chequagua Falls, which you can view from the foot of Main Street.

The Catharine Valley Trail follows the old Pennsylvania Railroad branch line.

From Montour Falls, southward to Horseheads, a rail-to-trail conversion of the old PRR branch line is underway. It is called the Catharine Valley Trail. A five-mile stretch is open (unpaved) between Montour Falls and Millport which is a great out-and-back ride. The on-road route is NY 14.

There are plans are to extend the Catherine Valley rail trail from Millport to Horseheads and the next stretch, including a bridge over NY 14, is under construction. The community organization, Friends of the Catherine Trail (see Resource Guide) is actively leading efforts to improve and expand this wonderful trail system. It's worth a ride.

The balance of the Chemung Canal path from Millport through

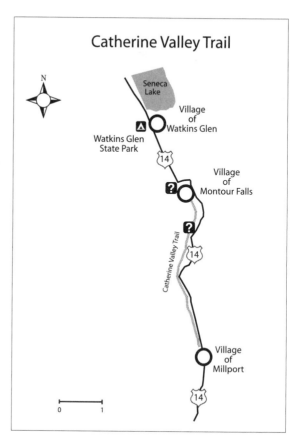

Horseheads and Elmira to Corning is very hard to follow and the roads are busy. Just east of Corning, the canal entered the Chemung River at Port Gibson — this may very well be the farthest "port" ever founded on the vast New York State canal system. In addition, beyond Elmira to the southeast, a privately-financed canal was built in 1854 alongside the Chemung River. Eleven wooden locks and two aqueducts were constructed. This canal was closed in 1871, sold to the Lehigh Valley Railroad, and tracks remain atop the old canal bed today. However, until the Caroline Trail is extended, I suggest that you avoid riding south to the Elmira/Corning area. If your long-distance goal is to reach New York's "Bike 17" in Elmira, you should contact local bicycle clubs for route advice; you can locate them through the links on the New York Bicycle Coalition website.

Crooked Lake Canal

The Crooked Lake Canal connected Seneca Lake, at Dresden, with Keuka Lake, at Penn Yan. In about seven miles, it climbed almost 300 feet to the 709-foot elevation of Keuka Lake utilizing twenty-eight locks. The canal was built along the north bank of the Keuka Outlet stream. By connecting to Keuka Lake, canal builders extended the reach of the Erie Canal system another twenty-two miles to Hammondsport. In the 1880s, a railroad was built alongside the canal and stream; it has been converted into an off-road trail called the Keuka Lake Outlet Trail. Developed and maintained by a volunteer group called the Friends of the Outlet, the path passes by three of the earliest settlements and mill sites in the region.

Louis Rossi

The Keuka Lake Outlet Trail follows the path of the old Penn Yan and New York Railway Company railroad.

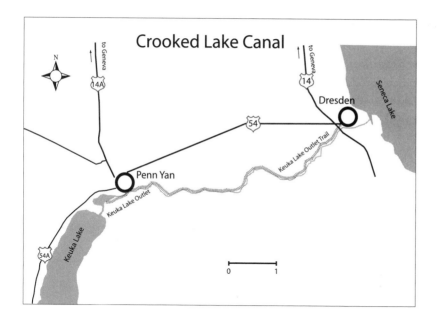

To reach this trail, you can either start at Dresden on Seneca Lake or Penn Yan on Keuka Lake. You will find the start of the canal on your way north from Watkins Glen or you can take a beautiful bike ride south from Geneva on NY 14 about thirteen miles.

The Keuka Lake Outlet Trail begins just east of NY 14 in Dresden. It extends seven and one-half miles, unpaved, to the outlet of Keuka Lake, adjacent to NY 54A in Penn Yan. This short trail has very good historical signage providing a great deal of information along the way; it is one of the best historically-signed trails I have seen. The most direct route back to Geneva from Penn Yan is NY 14A. There are many county roads in this area that offer quieter, but less direct routes.

Finalmente: "Il Giro D'Italy, New York"

As noted earlier, this part of New York has many similarities with the Italian countryside. Here is an interesting thirty-four mile loop ride that while not involving canals (the starting point, Penn Yan is at the summit of the Crooked Lake Canal) makes you feel like you're on a European vacation. I call it New York's "Giro d'Italia." Yes it's a "giro" or loop, through the village and town of Italy, New York. Italian immigrants were important to the early wine industry and many local spots carry Italian names. You could start and stop anywhere on this loop ("giro"), but making Penn Yan, the Yates County seat, one's base allows you to visit the Yates County Visitor's Center on NY 14A in Penn Yan for the latest tourism information and advice.

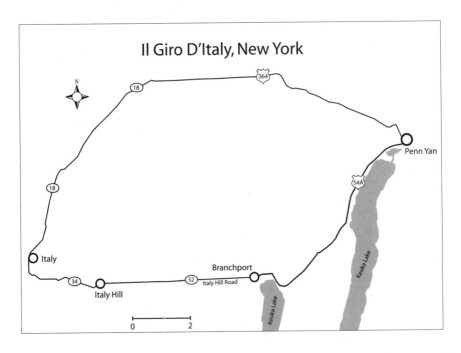

Il Giro D'Italy, New York

Penn Yan

Branchport

Italy

Italy Hill Road

Italy Hill

Keuka Lake

Keuka Lake

0   2

Depart Penn Yan on NY 54A and in eight miles arrive in Branchport. You'll be riding alongside Keuka Lake, another of New York's glacial Finger Lakes. Keuka has an unusual "Y-shape" caused by the merging of two glaciers. The only other glacial lake with this feature is Lago di Como in Italy. At Branchport, go straight ahead ("diritto") onto CR 32 Italy Hill Road. This is a long climb. Along this road, you'll enter the town of Italy. Continue straight. At the junction of Italy Friend Road go left and soon you will cycle through the small hamlet of Italy Hill. Immediately turn right onto CR 34, Italy Turnpike. After a big descent, turn right on CR 18, Italy Valley Road. Just four miles from the hamlet of Italy Hill, you'll come to the town's center, a total of sixteen miles from the start in Penn Yan. There is a small town hall and historical center. Continue straight through the on CR 18. Along this road you'll leave the town of Italy and come to NY 364, after a total ride of twenty-six miles. Turn right and you'll go back to Penn Yan, in a total of thirty-four miles or so. Molto Bene.

Louis Rossi

The historic Italy Town Hall is 16 miles from Penn Yan on Il Giro D'Italy, NY loop.

While the Erie Canal is recognized worldwide as a political and engineering triumph, the network of New York canals that was based upon the Cayuga-Seneca Canal and extended through the Finger Lakes Region is another very impressive accomplishment. It is one of the prettiest parts of New York State and great for an on-road cycling tourist. This chapter has described some tours that will quickly guide you to all the important sites along the Cayuga-Seneca Canal as well as to its entire extensive feeder network. If you rush, you can see it all in about five days, but there is so much to see — not just canal history, but magnificent glacial scenery, over fifty great vineyards, countless pretty towns and cities, and much more. There are so many high-quality state and local roads that the cycling opportunities here are almost limitless.

Because of the cliffs surrounding the south end of Cayuga Lake, building a canal southward from Ithaca would have been very difficult. In 1828, (two years before the charter of the Baltimore & Ohio Railroad) local Ithaca visionaries applied to the state legislature for a charter to build a thirty-five mile railroad which would extend the reach of the canal southward from Ithaca to the Susquehanna River at Owego. This was another of the very first railroads in America that you will find in Upstate New York. It was opened in 1834. This became part of the Delaware, Lackawanna & Western Railroad (DL&W) in 1855 and was DL&W's northern terminus for almost fifty years. DL&W was the nation's largest hauler of anthracite coal, which at the time was the principal source of home heating fuel. DL&W transshipped its coal from rail cars onto the canal network here in Ithaca. From here, anthracite coal moved north by barge across all of New York and on to Canada. Very late in the 19th century DL&W built its own rail mainline northward and westward to Buffalo and its route into Ithaca was abandoned. The active rail line you see today is a Lehigh Valley (LV) branch line that once extended to Lake Ontario. Like the DL&W, LV used these lines to move its anthracite coal northward.

Cycling off-road in western New York is great. Here, a rider enjoys the Riverwalk in Erie County. Photo: Ken Field

The Canals of Western New York

Cycling western New York crosses territory that was essentially outside, or beyond, the frontiers of both the Dutch colony of Nieuw Amsterdam and the British colony of New York. The French considered this region part of "New France." After all, they had discovered and settled the Saint Lawrence and Mississippi River basins, and the waterways of this part of upstate New York flowed north into the Saint Lawrence, "their" river.

After the French and Indian Wars, the British government had prohibited settlement "...beyond the Allegheny mountains." However, in this part of New York, there was no mountain barrier and the soils were especially fertile — so settlement continued. Since no natural waterways extended east-to-west completely across western New York (the principal drainage pattern is south-to-north), canal builders had to create an entirely land-locked waterway — a great 150-mile long engineering achievement.

The Erie Canal rose 178 feet from Lock 53 at Clyde in Wayne County to Lock 71 at Lockport in Niagara County — eighteen locks in all. Many aqueducts were required to cross over the north-flowing rivers, streams, and creeks. Today's barge canal uses ten locks (Lock 25 at Clyde to Lock 35 at Lockport) to accomplish the same climb.

The route chosen by the original canal builders is almost exactly the route of the present barge canal. As a result, almost all of the original horse/mule towpath alignment was preserved as an access way to the now-motorized barge canal. This kept the historic towpath intact and makes possible a wonderful off-road cycling experience.

From Palmyra to Tonawanda, on Buffalo's doorstep, all alignments of the Erie Canal follow one course. This is the easiest part of the canal to see. The route chosen by the original canal builders is exactly the course today. These were wise men. You'll see the Great Embankment, where the canal sails seventy feet above the Irondequoit Valley, the Genesee Aqueduct, one of the most historic bridges in the world, the awesome flight of locks at Lockport, and the Great Cut, where the canal cuts through the last ridge of the Niagara Escarpment. There are fascinating sites to see and this section will help you get there.

There are many boat tours that you can combine with cycling. If you take a boat trip, it will be on the original route of the canal. Perhaps the greatest wonder is how the canal, still, is a vibrant, living part of the many small towns and villages through which it flows. You'll enjoy the many canal towns along the way — they really know how to celebrate their canal.

Here in western New York, biking the Canalway Trail and its local components is a unique and great experience. Close-by is our old friend Bike "5," which pretty much follows NY 31 and is closely adjacent to the Erie. So on-road bicycling close to the canal is highly practical. Navigating the Erie by bike couldn't be easier.

Finally, in addition to the Erie Canal, the Genesee Valley Canal stretched 125 miles south from Rochester (and the Erie Canal) all the way into Pennsylvania. Its summit level was at 1489 feet near Cuba and 114 locks were built along this route. This canal passed through Letchworth Gorge, the "Grand Canyon of New York," and a cycle tour here will be quite an experience.

This region was the original western territory of the Five Nations that made up the Haudenosaunee. The Seneca Nation was the westernmost tribe and guarded the Western Door of the symbolic Longhouse that extended across New York. Ganondagan, the principal Seneca community, sat on a hilltop at the western edge of the natural waterways that made the powerful Five Nation Confederacy possible.

Chapter 16

Wayne County

Wayne County, which lies largely within original Seneca territory, is especially interesting from a geological perspective. For example, there are at least 150 cobblestone buildings in the county — out of less than a thousand nationwide. The cobbles are the result of beach erosion along the shore of ancient glacial Lake Iroquois 10,000 years ago. Pioneer farmers picked their crops of rocks each year and the stones were used to construct the landmark cobblestone buildings you will cycle by. The other glacial feature, mentioned earlier, is the vast fields of drumlins that are dramatic to look at but challenging hills to cycle across. If you stay on the Canalway Trail or Bike "5," you'll pass between them.

You will enter Wayne County from the east on Bike "5," which is NY 31. Bike "5" and the Erie Canal run side-by-side across most of Wayne County. Bike "5" stays atop NY 31, an excellent roadway for cycling and fulfills its role as your guide to the Erie Canal.

NY 31 is easy to follow and is in excellent condition. Traffic volumes are low and there are wide shoulders throughout. You have to use Bike "5" from the eastern border of Wayne County to Newark, for twenty-three miles. Along the way, you'll encounter historic Erie Canal sites and some bikeable disconnected segments of old towpath. At Newark you have the choice of staying on Bike "5," or riding on a new crushed limestone section of the Canalway Trail. From Newark, the Canalway Trail is complete and continuous the fourteen miles to the Monroe County border, and continues on all the way to the Niagara River. It is a wonderful resource for cyclists, and gets better each year.

Bike "5" passes directly through charming farm villages like Savannah, Clyde, Lyons, Newark, Port Gibson, Palmyra, and Macedon. The area between Rochester and Syracuse, in Wayne, Seneca, and Cayuga, offers some of the

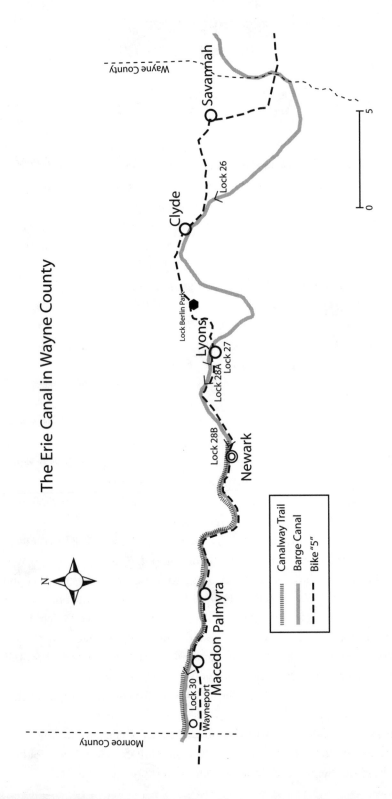

The Erie Canal in Wayne County

Wayne County

Savannah

Lock 26

Clyde

Lock Berlin Park

Lyons

Lock 27

Lock 28A

Lock 28B

Newark

Macedon Palmyra

Lock 30

Wayneport

Monroe County

N

Canalway Trail
Barge Canal
Bike "5"

0   5

NY 31 in Wayne County is an excellent road for cycling.

best roadways in New York State for cycling. Find a small town to stay in and don't hesitate to explore.

An observant cycle-historian will notice that in the eastern portion of Wayne County the original Erie Canal and today's barge canal alignments do differ a bit. Essentially, this is because the barge canal was placed into an "enlarged" Clyde River, which the original canal did not utilize. Here, like everywhere else across New York, the old Erie was completely in a land-locked canal bed, totally separate from rivers and streams.

There are many hidden Erie Canal treasures along the way. Between Clyde and Lyons, look for a small sign "Canal Park." It is visible in both directions. This will take you to Wayne County's Black Brook Area Canal Park, where there is good interpretive material on canal history and some stretches of well-maintained towpath for you to cycle. Less than a mile west on Bike "5" is Wayne County's Lock Berlin Area Canal Park. It also has a well-maintained grassy towpath for cycling. If you are riding high-pressure tires, you'll need to stay on Bike "5," but be sure to stop and see the old canal structures. If you are comfortable cycling on a hard, grassy surface, you'll be able to tour some of this hidden towpath.

The barge canal has some interesting stopping places. There is a pretty canal side park in Lyons at Barge Canal Lock 27. Lock 28, one mile west of Lyons, is right alongside Bike "5." This is the western maintenance hub for the Erie Canal and you might see barges or tugs in dry-dock. An old Erie Canal lock lies just a bit west alongside Dry Dock Road.

Heading west at Newark, you have two good choices. You can choose to stay on Bike "5" or ride west on the Canalway Trail. The Canalway Trail resumes at Erie Barge Canal Lock 28B. This is the start of the longest continuous stretch of the trail and extends almost all the way to Lake Erie, almost 125 miles away. Most of it

Wayne County Park at Lock Berlin has excellent interpretive data.

is unpaved but kept in excellent condition. The riding surface of the unpaved towpath is hard enough to support almost any bicycle type including high-pressure tires. Lock 29 in Macedon has interesting old Erie Canal structures right alongside.

Palmyra, the birthplace of the Mormon religion (The Church of Jesus Christ of Latter-day Saints), is of special interest. According to Mormon tradition, it was here, in AD 421, that Moroni, last survivor of an ancient people, buried the Mormon record, which was revealed by the Angel Moroni to Joseph Smith in 1820. The Joseph Smith home and many other important Mormon sites make worthwhile visits. A Hill Cumorah Pageant takes place every July. Hill Cumorah is an ice-age drumlin. Palmyra hosts special Canal Town Days in September.

At Palmyra, the Canalway Trail goes over the Palmyra Aqueduct. You can get a great photo of it from Bike "5."

The Canalway Trail runs 125 miles from Newark westward almost to Lake Erie.

You're cycling through some of the nation's best farmland.

Cycling across this portion of New York, you'll pass through some of the state's most fertile farmlands. In addition to dairying, you'll see extensive fruit crops. Not surprisingly, these fruit crops flourish due to glacial processes. The Great Lakes and the Finger Lakes, all glacial remnants, support a slightly warmer and dependable microclimate that is ideal for fruit. A fall trip, during the apple harvest season, can be spectacular. I've cycled this region with friends from the state of Washington, a state well known for its apple crop. They have marveled at the variety of apples grown in New York State — at least twenty-three varieties are available at one time or another during the growing season. The enormous Kraft Foods plant you'll ride by in Macedon indicates the use for much of New York's dairy production — the manufacture of cheese products. A helpful tool is the New York State Department of Agriculture and Markets "Guide to Farm Fresh Food," which may help direct you to fresh harvests.

I recommend that you ride the Canalway Trail west from Newark, through Palmyra, Macedon and Wayneport, to the border with Monroe County.

Ganondogan Historic Site

Before you head farther west, you may want to head south from Wayneport to the Ganondogan Historic Site. It is about ten miles off course, on a hilltop, south of the village of Victor. Ganondagan, the historic Western Door of the Haudenosaunee, sits atop a hilltop near Victor in Ontario County. This is a commanding location, like Ossernenon, the Eastern Door, and is well worth the out-and-back detour from the Canalway Trail.

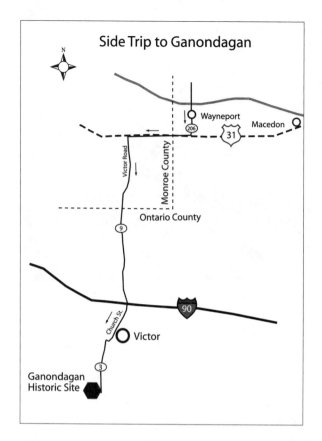

Side Trip to Ganondagan

N

Wayneport

206

Macedon

31

Victor Road

Monroe County

Ontario County

9

90

Church St.

Victor

Ganondagan
Historic Site

3

Getting out and back is easy. Leave the Canalway Trail at CR 206 in Wayneport. Head south to NY 31, which is Bike "5," and turn west (right) for a little over a mile. Take Victor Road which becomes CR 9. After crossing the New York State Thruway, bear right onto Church Street and pedal through the village of Victor to NY 96; it's a total of six miles between NY 31 and NY 96. In Victor, jog right on NY 96, then quickly left continuing south on Maple Street, which becomes Boughton Hill Road, CR 3. It's just a mile and one-half from Victor to the site of Ganondagan.

Archeologists have identified nearly thirty Seneca sites nearby. Grassy self-guided trails wind through the Ganondogan State Historic Site. Why not tie up the bikes and walk the trails?

It is about thirty-seven miles across Wayne County on Bike "5" or the Canalway Trail. You might consider an out-back ride using Bike "5" in one direction and the Canalway Trail segments returning, stopping at one or more of the parks along the way for lunch. Wayne County offers many canal exploring options.

Haudenosaunee — the "Western Door"

The British knew the Haudenosaunee as the Five Nations, subsequently as the Six Nations, and to the French as the Iroquois. If you consider a symbolic Longhouse stretching along your cycling route, the "Eastern Door," Ossernenon, was guarded by the Mohawks, and the "Western Door," Ganondagan, was guarded by the Senecas. The Onondaga were the "…keepers of the central hearth…"

The story of the Haudenosaunee is a rich one. Both the Dutch and British recognized the Haudenosaunee as an independent nation adjacent to their colony of Nieuw Amsterdam. Sir William Johnson, Baronet of New York and the King's ambassador to the Indians, married into the Mohawk tribe and fathered many Mohawk children. The Haudenosaunee alliances were indispensable to the British defeat of the French in North America. Haudenosaunee Chiefs traveled to and from England and met with British Royalty. The Haudenosaunee Confederacy played major roles in shaping American government — both the Articles of Confederation and the Constitution of the United States.

The powerful Huron and Iroquois Indian nations, who lived in these vast lands, had been at war long before the arrival of the French in Canada and the British and Dutch in America. Foolishly, Samuel de Champlain allowed himself to be drawn into these conflicts. Goaded by their Huron Indian allies, the French had been battling with the Iroquois since the day the first Frenchman, de Champlain, set foot in New York. In 1609, just months before Henry Hudson arrived on the Upper Hudson, de Champlain had fought a successful battle against the Iroquois near present day Ticonderoga. Ironically, his victory was a strategic defeat for the French.

In 1687, the French, under de Denonville destroyed the village of Ganondogan. Since he could not vanquish the Seneca, de Denonville devastated their lands. His reports state that he burned storehouses with about 500,000 bushels of corn. The Seneca later attacked Montreal in retaliation and the Iroquois allied themselves with the British. The Iroquois nation's defeat would ultimately come from the successful American forces who punished them for supporting the British in the Revolution. Most had stayed loyal to the British to the end. In an embarrassment to many loyal British citizens, the Treaty of Paris, which settled the Revolutionary War, made no provision for their defeated Iroquois allies. Many relocated in Canada after punitive raids by American forces destroyed their villages and crops. Subsequently, Jay's Treaty of 1794 provided some relief to the Iroquois.

The story of the Haudenosaunee stretches over some 800 years. Two great histories — Erie Canal and Indian — are linked in many ways. Threaded throughout this book are vignettes that tie them together. Your bicycle tour will visit many of the common sites that comprise this close relationship.

Chapter 17

Monroe County

*Monroe County offers many things for the canal tourist. On the
Erie, there are several striking canal sites: the Great Embankment
soaring seventy feet above the countryside and the Genesee
Aqueduct, surely one of the most historic bridges in the world.
Additionally, you can connect with the 90-mile Genesee Valley
Trail and follow that historic canal route.*

You should be entering Monroe County atop the Canalway Trail.
The trail is complete across Monroe County with a mixture of paved
and unpaved segments throughout. Bike "5" continues westward along
NY 31, however, be aware that it follows busy streets and is not suitable for
all cyclists.

Fairport and the neighboring village, Pittsford, are leaders in efforts
to make their canal facilities attractive. Fairport has three canalside parks:
Kennelley Park, Packett's Landing Wharf on the south bank of the canal,
and the North Bank Canal Park. All are good stopping or starting points.

Heading west from Fairport, you'll come to the Great Embankment where
the canal was elevated seventy feet above the surrounding countryside to
cross the Irondequoit Creek Valley. This one-mile route was one of the great
engineering achievements of James Geddes, who was not an engineer. Geddes
is responsible for discovering that the Genesee River, which would have to
be used to supply water to the canal, was in fact high enough to fill a level
embankment that hugged the ridge of the Irondequoit Valley. His achievement
was this great level embankment that made an inland canal route feasible.
Geddes later wrote:

> *While traversing these snowy hills in December 1808, I little thought of
> ever seeing the Genesee waters crossing this valley on the embankment now
> constructing over it. I had, to be sure, lively presentiments, that time would*

bring about all I was planning, that boats would one day pass along on the tops of these fantastic ridges, that posterity would see and enjoy the sublime spectacle, but that for myself, I had been born many, very many years too soon. (Quoted from: *Stars on the Water,* Condon)

Travel Tip

Should you wish to ride on-road in Monroe County, get the "Greater Rochester Area Bike Map," which is available from the Genesee Transportation Council. This is the best of all the urban maps in upstate New York and offers fair bicycle-safety ratings of all local streets. See Resource Section.

Pittsford is another lovely canal community that was once a busy shipping port with produce being sent to eastern markets. It also grew when the Auburn and Rochester railroad arrived in 1842. Check out Schoen Place with its shops and restaurants.

Just west of Pittsford, as you approach Lock 32, the barge canal diverges from the alignment of the original Erie Canal that extended through downtown Rochester; the alignments rejoin west of the city. The Canalway Trail continues along the barge canal. A short stretch of unimproved, unpaved bike path extends along the old canal bed to a park at old Erie Lock 62, a short interesting diversion.

The Erie Canalway Trail follows the barge canal, past Barge Canal Lock 32 (also the site of a small park) and does not enter downtown Rochester. Lock 33 is the last lock on the barge canal until Lockport. It begins another Long Level and is the longest flat stretch on the present Erie barge canal. Both Lock 32 and 33 have steep stairways so use caution if you're visiting them.

Follow the Erie Canalway Trail alongside the barge canal, do not use Bike "5" through Rochester.

Louis Rossi

The kiosk in Fairport is typical of those on the Canalway Trail. Note the lift bridge in the background.

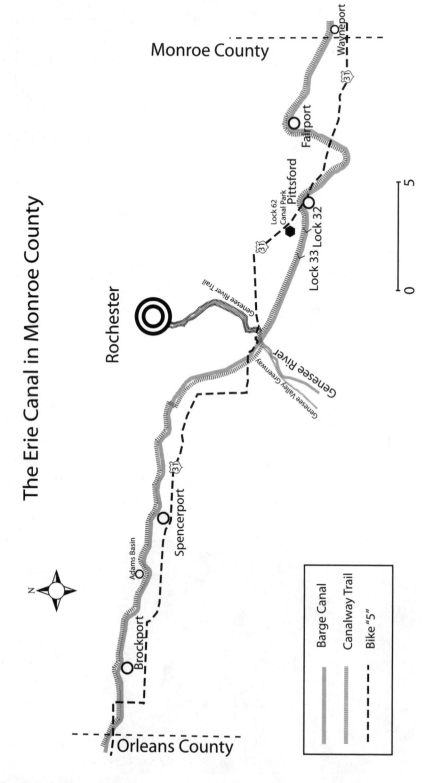

The Erie Canal in Monroe County

Monroe County

Wayneport

Fairport

Pittsford

Lock 62

Canal Park

Lock 33 Lock 32

Rochester

Genesee River Trail

Genesee Valley Greenway

Genesee River

31

Spencerport

Adams Basin

Brockport

N

Orleans County

Barge Canal

Canalway Trail

Bike "5"

5

0

The Canalway Trail meets a couple of trails in Genesee Valley Park, adjacent to the Genesee River. The paved Genesee River Trail heads north about three miles to downtown Rochester and seven more to Lake Ontario. (You can make a short loop.) A more challenging ride, the unpaved ninety-mile Genesee

The Great Embankment between Fairport and Pittsford is an engineering triumph.

Valley Greenway, extends southward. The Greenway follows the Genesee Canal, which once extended all the way to the Allegheny River at Olean, near the Pennsylvania border. This is a great ride and is covered in detail in the next chapter.

Visiting Rochester

Rochester is the home of corporate giants like Kodak, Bausch & Lomb, and Xerox. Monroe County leads New York in international trade. Indeed, Monroe County alone exports more goods than most states. That is what the Empire State was once all about. The original Erie Canal did go through the heart of Rochester, like it did in downtown Syracuse. You can visit the Genesee Aqueduct, which carried the Erie Canal over the Genesee River. This was the second largest aqueduct on the canal system (800 feet long with 10 stone arches) and the only one totally intact.

The Genesee Aqueduct is truly one of the most historic stone arch bridges in the world. It carried the Erie Canal across the Genesee River for some seventy years. It was so strongly built that, after the Erie Barge Canal was rerouted south of Rochester, the Aqueduct was converted into a highway and railroad viaduct. An electrified freight railroad "subway" once ran in the old canal bed and was used to interchange freight among all the railroads that served busy industrial Rochester until 1997. Today, the aqueduct carries Broad Street, a major commercial thoroughfare, across the Genesee River.

From above, it is impossible to tell that you are cycling over an original Erie aqueduct. However from an adjacent bridge you'll be very impressed to see the old aqueduct beneath today's Broad Street.

Just a few blocks north of Broad Street, just beyond the New York Central (CSX and AMTRAK) railroad overpass is Brown's Race, a new urban park. From Brown's Race, you can bike out onto a bike and pedestrian viaduct the overlooks the Genesee Falls. George Washington visited these falls and commissioned four large artworks to hang in his new dining room at Mount Vernon. One was a painting of these falls.

Continuing west along the Canalway Trail, the Greece Town Park makes a good rest stop. Once ready to roll again, travel west through Spencerport, Adams Basin, and Brockport. Spencerport celebrates Fireman's Days in June and Canal Days in July. The Fireman's Day parade draws 10,000 spectators to this small village — it is one of the largest fireman's parades in upstate New York.

Notice the bridge carrying Union Street over the canal in Spencerport. This, and fifteen more just like it in western New York, is a unique lift bridge. When a boat passes, the bridge lifts to permit the boat to pass beneath. Take note of the pedestrian walkways. When these structures were built, special accommodations were made so that pedestrians (and bicyclists) would not be disrupted by boat traffic. In its raised position, the bridge deck realigns itself with stairways and becomes an elevated walkway. The New York Department of Transportation has restored this and many other bridges like it. They

The original Erie Canal Aqueduct across the Genesee River is still in use today, though it carries cars, not canal boats, in downtown Rochester.

As you arrive at another attractive and historic lock side canal park, let's step back a moment and describe how these parks came to be. After all, there are over thirty on the Erie Canal and over twenty more on the other operating canals. What you see today is a very minor touch of the far-reaching hand of New York's Governor Nelson A. Rockefeller. With the possible exception of De Witt Clinton, no governor played a greater role in shaping New York State than Nelson Rockefeller. By 1970, the canals were in need of major repair. Additionally, the commercial role of the canals was declining. Should they be closed? In a minor act of brilliance, the Rockefeller Administration recognized that the canals would have to focus on a recreational role in the future, if they were to be saved. Special funds were made available in 1971 and the first lock parks were built by the Department of Transportation that same year. The parks were an immediate success and started a stream of recreational improvements that continue to this day.

deserve a special compliment for their careful treatment and respect for these historic structures.

Just west of Spencerport is the small hamlet of Adams Basin. Adjacent to another of the sixteen wonderful lift bridges over the Erie Canal is the Canalside Inn. If you saw Putnam's Store at Yankee Lock in Montgomery County or Sims Store in Onondaga County, you saw a museum of an old-time canal store. The Canalside Inn, a Bed & Breakfast today, is a living canal building, and the most interesting of the three. The oldest parts of the inn date from the construction of the Erie Canal. The interiors are perfectly preserved.

New York State Canal Commission

Greece Canal Park. Many canal municipalities have police patrols on bikes.

Brockport is the last Monroe County village you'll hit heading west on the Canalway Trail. It is home to a major campus of the State University of New York and a thriving bedroom community for Rochester. If you wish to cycle on-road, you can pick up Bike "5," in Brockport and follow it west. But there are many quiet, local roads closer or adjacent to the canal that you may also find attractive for cycling.

Whether on or off-road, soon you will come to the border of Monroe and Orleans counties. It is forty miles across Monroe County on the Canalway Trail.

The Canalside Inn in Adams Basin with a lift bridge in the raised position.

A lift bridge allows pedestrians to cross when the bridge is up.

Chapter 18

The Genesee Canal

The Genesee Valley Canal stretched 125 miles south from the Erie Canal in downtown Rochester to the Allegany River near the Pennsylvania border. By reaching the upper Allegany River, canal builders created an important linkage between the Erie Canal and the Ohio River at Pittsburgh. Construction was authorized in 1836. By 1841, the canal was open to Dansville, fifty-two miles away and a climb of a mere 174 feet. The difficult task was ahead. Fifty locks (Locks #11 to #60) would be required in just nineteen miles to climb to an 1132-foot level. And yet another thirty-seven locks would be required to reach the 1489-foot summit level at Cuba. Then the canal descended to the Allegany River at Olean, 107 miles from Rochester, at an elevation of 1422 feet. All this was completed by 1862. By this time, rail transportation had become far more efficient over hilly, if not mountainous terrain such as this, and the Genesee Canal closed to traffic in 1878 — a very short life span indeed.

A great deal of the old canal towpath has been opened for bicycling and hiking — between Rochester and Cuba, more than seventy-five miles of unpaved, off-road trail lies atop the old canal bed. Called the Genesee Valley Greenway, the trail is perfect for off-road mountain bikes, but too rough for narrow-tired road bikes. However, on-road bike tourists and explorers will find excellent local roads to follow the course of the canal. Although there is no numbered bike route to guide you, there are many good options to choose from.

The Genesee Valley Canal passed through the southern end of Letchworth Gorge. Seeing the gorge, among many other reasons, makes a cycle trip here worthwhile. Unlike many of the other canals of New York, the Genesee was rural — and the area remains that way. There are no big cities along the way, only pastoral scenes that make exploring this canal a delight.

The Genesee Valley Greenway

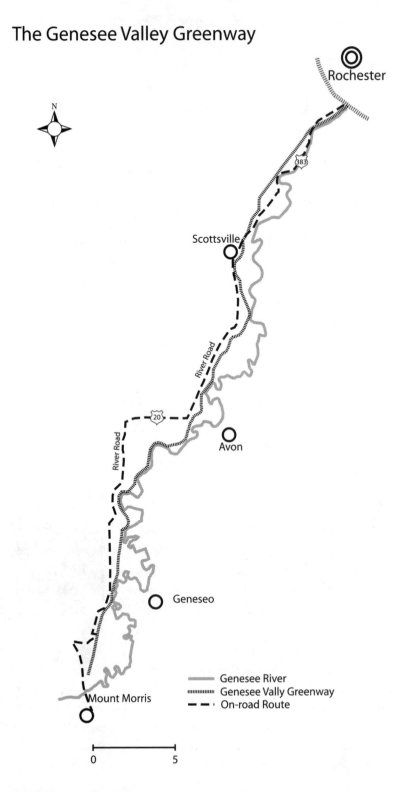

Rochester

383

Scottsville

River Road

20

River Road

Avon

Geneseo

Genesee River
Genesee Vally Greenway
On-road Route

Mount Morris

0   5

Following the Genesee Valley Canal is a multi-day venture. Probably New York's most successful trail project, the Genesee Valley Greenway makes this one of the easiest canals to uncover. The Friends of the Genesee Valley Greenway is truly an impressive volunteer group. Check out their website (See the Resource Guide) to find the latest trail information, maps, photos, descriptions, and for the opportunity to get a question answered.

Then, after the railroad was abandoned in the mid-twentieth century, a utility company, Rochester Gas & Electric, preserved its route. Finally, just a few years ago, the company sold the corridor back to the state. So, while it is a complex story with many histories, we are very fortunate to see this historic route come full circle. It is today one of the very best preserved, long-distance, off-road trails in New York. It is almost 100 percent unpaved and conditions vary. There are gaps in some spots, especially river crossings, but nearly all of the 113 miles of the old canal are open to explore — quite an accomplishment.

The Genesee River flows south-to-north from Pennsylvania all the way to Lake Ontario. Once a major thoroughfare of the powerful Seneca Nation, it became an integral part of the design of the Erie Canal. It fills the Erie Canal across the Great Embankment high above the Irondequoit Valley and provides water eastward from Rochester all the way to Montezuma. The present barge canal still relies on Genesee waters that now flow all the way to Oswego on the Oswego Canal.

Louis Rossi

The Genesee Greenway Trail is great for hybrid and mountain bikes.

fter closing in 1878, most of the Genesee Valley Canal was sold by the state and converted into a railroad (a branch line of the Pennsylvania Railroad) back in the late nineteenth century. Like many of the railroads you've encountered elsewhere, the PRR used this line to move coal (soft, bituminous coal) northward. Anthracite coal, which is only found in eastern Pennsylvania, was once the main source of home heating fuel throughout the northeastern United States and Canada. Bituminous coal, much more common and cheaper, was an industrial fuel. The PRR brought this coal to the industries of Rochester.

Rochester to Mount Morris

Our story begins near the historic Broad Street Aqueduct where the Erie Canal crossed the Genesee River. From here, back in 1836, the Genesee Valley Canal extended south, along the west side of the river. The first fifty miles was a fairly flat route, requiring only ten locks. You can ride, off-road, on the old canal bed south from downtown Rochester. Off-road segments are pretty continuous and where gaps exist, there are good signs linking the segments. It is a tour for off-road or hybrid bikes. For the on-road tourist, fortunately, local roads are quite good, and with a few good maps, an on-road cyclist can enjoy the tour as well. For on-road travel, you'll want to head south from the outskirts of Rochester on SR383, Scottsville Road. From Scottsville, where you'll find historic interpretive signage, head south on River Road, west a short distance on US 20, then south, again on River Road all the way to NY 36 and into Mount Morris.

Mount Morris to Portageville

Now things got tough for canal builders. From Lock 11, it took fifty-nine locks in just ten miles to climb 530 feet to the 1132-foot elevation at the top of Letchworth Gorge in Portageville. Perhaps this is the most interesting portion of the canal to tour. Portions of the off-road trailway are open, and there are fine local roads to follow the canal on-road.

To "climb" up the Genesee River, canal builders chose a detour to follow a more gradual climb along the Keshequa Creek. Near Sonyea, on NY 36, the Genesee Canal turned to follow the Keshequa, which meanders through the hamlets of Tuscarora, Coopersville, Nunda, and Oakland. This is a particularly beautiful part of New York, but tracing the old canal is not easy. There is a giant state prison at Sonyea that blocks the start of the route. And a lot of the canal bed has been lost due to erosion by the Keshequa Creek. To follow the canal on-road, leave NY 36 on Dutch Road; follow Dutch Road to Tuscarora where some historic canal sites are evident. Then follow Scipio Road south to Nunda-Mt Morris Road; follow it to NY 408, State Street, into Nunda. At Nunda, turn west on NY 436. After Oakland, you will come alongside a well-preserved flight of locks that climbs to the summit-level at Portageville. Along the way, you will find open stretches of the Genesee Valley Greenway trail that can be used. These are unpaved and conditions vary with weather.

Letchworth State Park Loop

The north end of Letchworth State Park is thirty-five miles south of Rochester. The seventeen-mile long park itself is so awesome that a loop ride in this area is well worth the effort. With a base in Mount Morris or in Letchworth Park, a loop of about forty miles will give you an outstanding tour through the park, between Portageville and Mount Morris as well as a good tour of the Genesee Canal's most interesting sites on the way back. The park contains an enormous gorge, called "The Grand Canyon of the East." You'll find three waterfalls with a cumulative fall of 600 feet, pools, cabins, campsites, the famous Glen Iris Inn, a museum, and many hiking trails. Not all off-road trails in the park permit biking, but Trail #7 does. It is the old Genesee Canal towpath that takes you to the historic Genesee Canal locks near Oakland.

To ride a day trip to the best Genesee Canal sites and tour Letchworth Park, base yourself in Mt. Morris, thirty-five miles south of Rochester. From Mt. Morris, cycle south on NY 408 about eleven miles to Nunda. Here you can find open Genesee Valley Greenway trail segments that you can follow west to Portageville. To continue on-road, turn west (right) in Nunda on NY 436 and follow it uphill to Portageville. Be sure to stop at the flight-of-locks on your right. It is six miles by road to the entrance to Letchworth State Park. You can follow "Trail #7" from the top of the locks, off-road, into the park at Portageville. Once you've entered the park, you have a beautiful seventeen-

Be sure to stop at some of the overlooks at Letchworth Park.

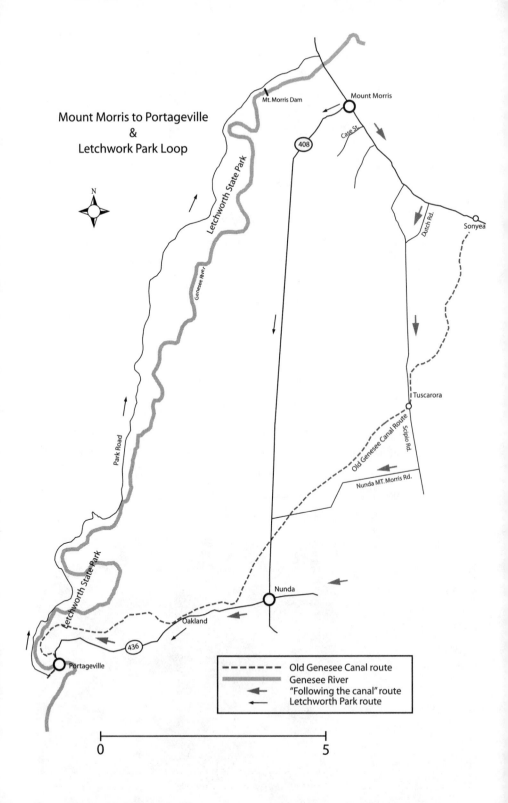

Mount Morris to Portageville
&
Letchwork Park Loop

N

Letchworth State Park

Mt. Morris Dam

Mount Morris

Case St.

408

Dutch Rd.

Sonyea

Genesee River

Tuscarora

Old Genesee Canal Route

Scipio Rd.

Nunda MT. Morris Rd.

Park Road

Nunda

Letchworth State Park

Oakland

436

Portageville

- - - - Old Genesee Canal route
—— Genesee River
← "Following the canal" route
← Letchworth Park route

0   5

Louis Rossi

You can observe ruins of Genesee Canal locks from Oakland to Portageville alongside NY 436.

mile on-road ride with some challenging climbs back to Mt. Morris. This section has dozens of scenic overlooks and rest stops; take your time and enjoy.

As you near the finish of the park road (and a nice downhill run), you'll come to the Mt. Morris Dam that is worth a visit. Then you'll emerge on NY 36, just one mile north of your starting point for the loop. This forty-mile loop offers the opportunity to see some of the best-preserved Genesee Canal sites, as well as the opportunity to bike through one of New York's most scenic state parks.

Primal Pictures

A massive flood control dam protects Mt. Morris.

The flight of Genesee Canal locks between Oakland and Portageville are impressive. This is a very well-preserved portion of the sixty locks it took to make this dramatic 530-foot climb in roughly ten miles. There are many historical, interpretative signs to help you understand how the canal was built and operated as well as the commercial role it played.

There is one minor error in the signage. Because the climb consisted of single-lock chambers (not double lock like the Erie Canal), arrangements had to be made to allow boats going up and down to pass one another, otherwise the delays would have been lengthy. To facilitate this, "double-wide" areas were built between the locks that permitted one boat to move aside and permit the other to pass. The historical markers incorrectly identify these wide areas as reservoirs.

Portageville to Cuba and Olean

Building south from Portageville, canal builders had a brief ten-mile respite, with a fairly flat route along the Genesee River. Then, to reach Olean and the Allegany River, they had to leave the Genesee Valley near Belfast and climb another 330 feet to the canal's summit level near Cuba. That brought the canal to 1489 feet in elevation. Locks 97 and 98 maintained each end of the summit level. Cuba Lake, 1665 feet above sea level, was built to supply water to the summit level. Today, Cuba Lake is a very popular boating spot. Finding enough water to keep the canal in business was quite a problem, and this reservoir was part of the solution. Its waters flowed both north and south down the Genesee Valley Canal. The north-flowing waters entered the Erie

Louis Rossi

Southern sections of the Greenway Trail can be rough but suitable for off-road bikes.

Canal near Rochester and flowed eastward. The south-flowing waters entered the Allegany River and would wind up going down the Mississippi to the Gulf of Mexico.

Portions of the Genesee Valley Trail are open in this region between Portageville and Cuba, but not as well-maintained as the more northerly segments. But given time, the volunteer groups that are dedicated to this trail will also have these sections in good shape.

On-road, the primary routes are NY 19A from Portageville to Fillmore, NY 19 from Fillmore to Belfast, NY 305 from Belfast to Cuba, NY 446 from Cuba to Hinsdale, NY 16 from Hinsdale to Olean, and NY 417 (Bike "17") from Olean to Millgrove. In some places, quiet, local roads parallel some of these stretches of good state highway as well.

The off-road Genesee Valley Trail ends near Cuba. There are no off-road options from here to Olean; you must ride on-road. Near Hinsdale, the canal began its descent to Olean, where it entered the Allegany at an elevation of 1422 feet.

A Special Note on Olean

Olean, itself, has some history worth citing. First, Olean's name is linked to the extensive oil deposits in this region of southwestern New York, northeastern Pennsylvania and northeastern Ohio. The Senecas used these oils for medicinal purposes. This is where the great Standard Oil fortune of the Rockefellers was made. In 1881, one of the first major oil pipelines in the world was built here by Standard Oil, linking Olean with the Hudson River in New Jersey. Second, the Erie Railroad (now a part of Norfolk Southern) is itself quite historic, having been completed from the Hudson River to Lake Erie in 1851; at the time it was hailed as "...the greatest continuous work of man since the Great Wall of China..." It was, indeed, an enormous accomplishment and offered an east-to-west commercial route to communities all across the "Southern Tier" of New York State in much the same way as the Erie Canal did to communities between Buffalo and Albany. The ceremonial "completion" of the Erie Railroad took place in Cuba, New York. With river-based transportation, the historic canal, the pipeline, and the Erie Railroad, Olean's transportation history is pretty rich indeed.

For perspective, Olean had the world's longest continuous railroad in 1851 (the Erie Railroad); was connected through the Genesee Canal, in 1867, to the Great Lakes and Atlantic Ocean; was linked to the Ohio River via the Allegany River; and had the word's longest oil pipeline in 1881.

Travel Tip
There are very good, high-quality intercity bus services that will take you eastward to other feeder canals or to Buffalo to rejoin the Erie Canal. See the Resource Guide..

From Olean, on the Allegany River, travelers and freight could boat or raft downstream to Pittsburgh and into the Ohio River. This is quite significant as it meant that the Erie Canal network had reached the Allegheny, Ohio, and ultimately the Mississippi rivers, opening a second vast gateway to the West.

The Genesee Valley Canal is a multi-day tour with the total time dependent on whether you ride on-road or on the trail, how many scenic stops you make, and your stamina. If you're coming from the Erie Canal, I suggest a ride from Rochester through Mount Morris and on to Letchworth Park, where you can camp or lodge. Take another day or two to complete the loop and return to Rochester. This is beautiful countryside and the combination of off-road and on-road options, and the magnificence of Letchworth Park, make this historic canal route a great cycling opportunity.

Chapter 19

Orleans County

You have the choice of Bike "5" (NY 31) or the Canalway Trail all the way across Orleans and then Niagara counties. On either route, you won't encounter any hills. Imagine finding a totally level line across a county. Now, imagine finding a level line across almost three counties. That's what the early canal engineers found and that is why there are no locks in Orleans County. The closest lock to the east is Lock 33 near Pittsford and the closest lock to the west is Lock 34 in Lockport. This Long Level, extending for over seventy miles, makes for wonderful cycling. For the most part, you are following the shoreline of ancient Lake Iroquois, a major glacial lake. The flat beach made this engineering trick possible.

Cycling westward through Orleans County, you will never be far from the shore of Lake Ontario; typically less than ten miles separates the lake from the canal. There are many state parks along the Lake Ontario shoreline and the Seaway Trail is a good cycling route, so feel free to experiment and add some attractive farm country, and maybe a swim, to your trip. Also, running parallel to the canal, just a bit to the north, is NY 104. Local folks call this "Ridge Road." The ridge is, indeed, the shoreline of the ancient glacial lake. First used by the Senecas and Iroquois, the trail was later developed into a stagecoach turnpike. Ridge Road is sometimes called "the road of the cobblestone houses," for it has more such buildings than on any highway in America.

Like Wayne and Monroe, Orleans County is real Erie Canal territory — the towns and villages are classic canal communities since the present canal follows the old alignment. It is also rich farmland, specializing in fruit crops. You'll need to cycle north or south of the canal to find the best farmlands.

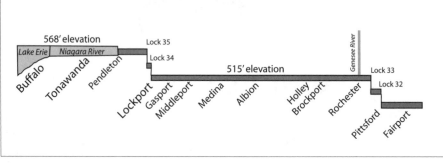

A profile of the western Erie Canal showing the Long Level.

Travel Tip

State Parks on the Lake Ontario Shore

New York State has an excellent park system along the Lake Ontario Shore between Rochester and Niagara Falls. Each of these parks offers something unique. As they are typically about ten miles north of the Canalway Trail in Monroe, Orleans, and Niagara counties, loops and detours to these sites are highly practical. Getting to-and-from these seven state parks, stretched for about sixty miles along the Lake Ontario shoreline, is really no more complex than picking a north-south local road of your own choice. But remember, the Long Level of the Erie Canal is tracing the old shoreline of ancient (glacial) Lake Iroquois at an elevation of 515 feet, and the level of Lake Ontario is 245 feet, so expect a climb or descent of 267 feet.

Park	Departure Point on Canalway Trail
Hamlin Beach State Park	Brockport
Oak Orchard State Park	Albion
Lakeside Beach State Park	Albion
Golden Hill State Park	Middleport
Wilson-Tuscarora State Park	Lockport
Four-Mile Creek State Park	Lockport
Fort Niagara State Park	Lockport

For details on these parks (facilities, schedules, camping details, etc) it is best to go to the New York State Office of Parks and Recreation website.

The Canalway Trail and Bike "5" are close to each other in Orleans County.

There are three canal towns in Orleans County. While there are no locks in these towns to serve as your base for a daytrip, each village has an attractive canal park adjacent to the Erie Barge Canal.

First, you'll come to the village of Holley, named for an early canal commissioner, which owes its existence to the Erie Canal. The site of this village was originally covered with a heavy growth of hemlock trees that were mostly standing when the canal was surveyed. The village was settled about the time the original embankment was constructed. Holley recently expended over a million dollars to develop recreational trails adjacent to the canal which link to nearby sites. There is a Depot Museum in Holley that will explain some of the local rail history.

The villages of Albion and Medina are especially inviting because you can experience the canal in a small community context. Because the canal is on the original alignment and these well-kept villages are creations of the canal, you find a real Erie Canal ambiance. You might want to visit the Cobblestone Society Museum in Albion. The only cobblestone museum in the world, it showcases the unique masonry construction method using stones rounded and polished into cobble by glacial action.

Note the striking red-brown buildings of Medina, constructed of Medina Sandstone, a building material once in demand all over the country. Medina celebrates the canal with a Canal Festival each July.

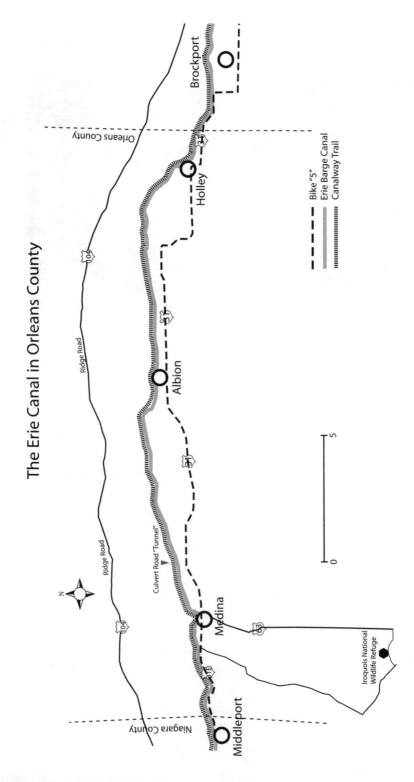

The Erie Canal in Orleans County

Brockport

Orleans County

Holley

Ridge Road

104

Albion

Ridge Road

Culvert Road "Tunnel"

Medina

Iroquois National
Wildlife Refuge

Niagara County

Middleport

Bike "5"
Erie Barge Canal
Canalway Trail

Culvert Road is the only roadway under the canal.

It was a level route across Orleans County for Erie Canal builders so there are no locks to see. However, seventeen miles into the county from the east, just before Medina at Culvert Road, there is something unique in all of New York. Here, the canal crosses over Culvert Road; both boats and bikes sail over the roadway traffic below. This is the only highway tunnel under the canal. This unique tunnel was a feature of the original Erie Canal and was retained when the expanded Erie Barge Canal was built. Be sure to bike under the canal, too. (Yes, it drips!)

The railroad you have been following is the Falls Road, first opened in 1837. Years ago, this formed an important New York Central system route from Rochester to Niagara Falls, across Canada to Detroit, and on to Chicago. Today, most of the Falls Road in New York and Canada is closed or serves only local traffic. Excursion trains run on weekends during the summer and foliage season.

If railroad history is of interest to you, stop at the handsome brick and stone depot on Main Street in Medina. There you'll find a flourishing railroad museum featuring one of the largest layouts in the nation, which when finished, will be an immense 204-foot long by 14-foot wide display.

Travel Tip

Just seven miles south of Medina is the Iroquois National Wildlife Refuge, a 10,000-acre site where you might see nesting bald eagles on a TV monitor at the visitors center or spot thousands of Canada geese on spring and fall migrations. Take NY 63 south and return on parallel local roads.

It is only twenty-four easy miles across Orleans County. You might consider a loop of a little over fifty miles by starting in Brockport in Monroe County, cycling up the Canalway Trail to Medina, stopping for lunch, and then returning on Bike "5."

Jim Cassatt

The model train layout at the railroad museum in Medina is worth a stop.

Chapter 20

Niagara County

Niagara County, a rich farmland, is one of the most cycle-friendly counties in New York State. There are excellent local roads and pretty villages as well as important history and world-famous scenery. Nearly ten million grapes are harvested here each year. Other fruit crops include apples, cherries, various berries, peaches, pears, plums, and prunes. There is a Peach Festival in Lewiston in September and an Apple Festival in Lockport in October.

I f you entered Niagara County on Bike "5" you will be on NY 31E, which ends in Middleport and joins NY 31. If you are following the Canalway Trail on top of the canal bed, you will arrive in Middleport as well. There you'll find a very large 1841 cobblestone landmark, the First Universalist Church, on South Main Street. The church's cobblestones were gathered at congregational picnics organized for this purpose.

Leaving Middleport on either route, you'll soon pass the pretty canal town of Gasport and come to Lockport, which is a must see for canal buffs. (These three ports tell us by their names that they were founded after the canal was built.) At Lockport, the final fifty-foot climb to the 565-foot elevation level of Lake Erie takes place.

The final climb is of the Niagara Escarpment, which is about 160-feet high in all and takes us above the shore of ancient, glacial Lake Iroquois to the level of modern Lake Erie. Once on top, it is a flat ride to Buffalo or Niagara Falls. There are no more locks.

The Barge Canal and Canalway Trail turn southwest and enter Erie County in the town of Amherst. Bike "5" continues directly west, along NY 31, to Niagara Falls. This presents a tough choice. One option is to make Lockport your base, cycle east one day through Orleans County and return to Lockport. The next day, make a loop to Niagara Falls and back. Finally, on a third day, a round-trip to Buffalo is practical.

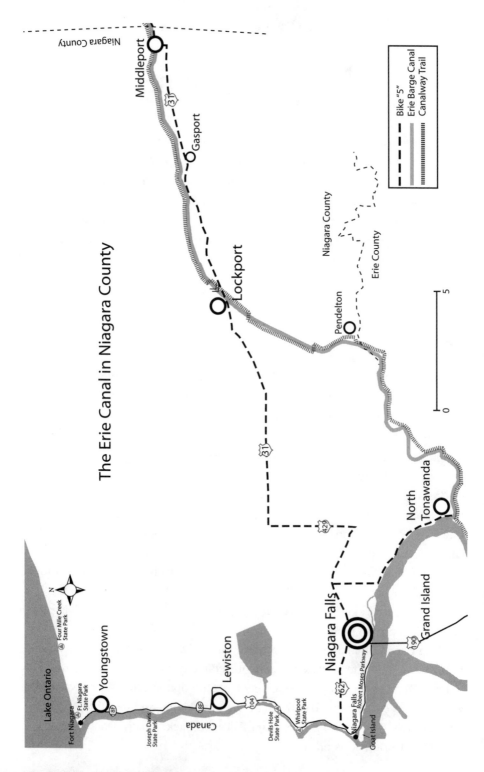

The Erie Canal in Niagara County

Legend:
- Bike "5"
- Erie Barge Canal
- Canalway Trail

*The flights of locks
at Lockport, old
and new, stand
side-by-side.*

Bike "5" will take you to the Rainbow Bridge almost adjacent to the falls. Make sure to visit the New York State Reservation on Goat Island. The many quiet vantage points on Goat Island offer the best perspectives of the falls and a bicycle is the best way to get around to all of them. There is so much to see along the Niagara River, in two countries, that you should plan to set aside at least a full day, perhaps two, for bicycle touring. While cycling in the Niagara Falls area, you might notice the Tuscarora Indian Reservation. Who are the Tuscaroras? These peoples are the sixth tribe to join the Five Nations, which is why many people refer to the Iroquois as "the Six Nations." The Tuscaroras were welcomed as full members of the league, but only arrived in New York

The original five locks of the Erie Canal and Locks 34 and 35 of the Barge Canal stand side-by-side in Lockport. This is a unique sight. Here, the difference between early 19th-century engineering and early 20th-century engineering stand starkly in contrast.

On the Barge Canal, Lock 35 is the final lock. The topmost lock on the old Erie Canal was Lock 71 but when first built, the original Erie Canal had 83 locks. Learn more about the history of these locks at a small Erie Canal Museum on the site.

A pproaching Locks 34 and 35 Lockport, the vertical rock walls rise abruptly on either side, revealing the jagged features of the canal's final challenge: the Niagara Escarpment. Five double-locks (ten stone lock-chambers in all, fifty-six feet tall) were built here from the start so that boats could ascend and descend without delay. These were the only double-locks on Clinton's Ditch. In addition, unlike any other flight of locks, each of the five up-and-down chambers carried its own independent plumbing so that any one of the five could be raised or lowered on its own. This may be unique in the world. All subsequent 19th century Erie Canal enlargements retained the original design as built on this spot. Then, in the 20th century, the Barge Canal replaced one side of the flight of five locks with two large barge-sized locks, each with a lift of 24.5 feet. The other half of the historic flight was retained and preserved. The old hydraulic powerhouse that once operated the city's locks and two lift bridges, is now a canal museum.

These complex stone structures were the very last piece of Clinton's Ditch to be completed — and once they were in place, Governor Clinton, in October of 1825, traveled the length of the canal in a packet boat, Seneca Chief, receiving accolades at every town.

in the early 1700s. By then, the Iroquois League was already very old. Our constitutional provisions permitting the entrance of new territory as equals to the thirteen original states comes from this action of the Haudenosaunee Confederacy.

If you visit the falls, you may want to complete your tour of important battlefield sites with a visit to Fort Niagara, twelve miles north, where the Niagara River enters Lake Ontario. Begun by the French at the time of La Salle, in 1679, the present fort dates from 1726. Fort Niagara was an important base of operations against American revolutionaries. It was used to arm and supply the Seneca and other Iroquois tribes who were fighting for the British. After the Revolution and after the destruction of their homes and farms by the Americans, many Iroquois relocated to the Niagara Frontier and settled on both sides of the river. Jay's Treaty of 1794 gave the Iroquois the free right to pass and repass across the national border. Indian tribes in New York, Ontario, and Quebec have this right to this day. Every year, in July an Indian Border Crossing Celebration takes place near Niagara Falls. There is an Indian parade across the border, unchecked by immigration officers, and many other celebrations of Indian rights and customs.

Niagara Falls is about twenty miles from Lockport. The visitors are standing on Goat Island, a good destination for bicyclists.

Niagara Falls, one of the great natural wonders of the world, is the last of the glacial Ice Age features that your tour will unveil to you. To recall a few — you started at Albany at a glacial *fjord* (Hudson River), passed through an ice-age *gap* that separated ancient Lakes Iroquois and Albany, saw glacial *potholes*, rode up and down glacial *drumlins*, saw countless *erratics*, viewed countless *cobblestone* landmarks, and now you've arrived at what is probably the world's largest ice-age waterfall. A waterfall as breathtaking as Niagara has a very short geologic life — perhaps 20,000 years. Some 10,000 have already gone by. In fact, when formed, the falls were seven miles downstream near today's Lewiston-Queenston Bridge. Left untouched by man, Niagara Falls would disappear into river rapids in another 10,000 years, retreating toward Buffalo at a rate of 3-5 feet per year. But the falls are now part of a magnificent international park and, through careful management and engineering, are likely to last a lot longer. They are an unforgettable sight.

It is about a fifteen-mile scenic ride on bike-safe roads to Fort Niagara from Niagara Falls. Almost adjacent to the Rainbow Bridge, on its north side, the Robert Moses Parkway resumes. One side of the four-mile section north of the Rainbow Bridge has been converted into a recreational pathway. You will truly enjoy cycling these four miles north along the Niagara Gorge, past many beautiful state parks. Then, you'll follow NY 104 approximately three and one-half miles to the intersection with NY 18F. While on NY 104 you'll ride by historic Niagara University and across a gigantic power dam where much of New York's electricity is generated. Then, you'll descend the Niagara Escarpment. Turn left on NY 18F and follow it through the attractive Village of Lewiston, past several more state parks, alongside the beautiful Niagara River, directly to the gates of old Fort Niagara, seven and one-half miles. James Fennimore's novel *The Pathfinder* accurately describes this old fort back in the early 1700s.

Fort Niagara played a major role in unsuccessful American invasions of Canada in the War of 1812. Captured by the British late in 1813, it may very well be the last piece of continental America to have been captured in warfare and occupied by a foreign power.

In retaliation for the American burning of the village of Niagara, the British put most of the American settlements along the Niagara to the torch. Instead of annexing Canada, the American invasions did much to encourage the small Canadian provinces to unify. Luckily, the fledgling American republic did not lose the War of 1812 to England, and peace was finally achieved on the border.

Let's get back to the central purpose of our tour, the Erie Canal, which went southwest from Lockport to Buffalo. Just west of Lockport, the canal enters the Great Cut. This rock cut extends for more than six miles and is about thirty feet deep. It is impressive today; imagine excavating it almost two hundred years ago.

To follow the Erie Canal to Buffalo, take the Canalway Trail, which links Lockport with Amherst in Erie County. This route closely follows the Great Cut, and has observation points to look down into this engineering triumph of the 18th century, which is still in use today. The trail is unpaved, with a stone-dust surface as far as Pendleton.

If you prefer to ride on-road, you are somewhat on your own, but following the canal is not difficult. First, in Lockport find State Road along the south embankment of the canal, just off Bike "5" at Transit Street. Take State Road to Summit Street. Make a jog across the canal and turn again to follow the canal's other embankment along Bear Ridge Road. When you come to Lockport Road (Robinson Road), cross back again over the canal to East Canal Road. Follow East Canal Road. You will arrive in Pendleton, which lies on the border of Niagara County. All the time, the canal will be adjacent to you. Look for the large guard gates that can be used to close the canal. Every winter they are lowered and the canal is drained and repaired. Cross the Tonawanda Creek and enter Erie County. It is only six miles from Lockport to the Erie County border. This is not as difficult as it sounds.

In total, it is thirty-two miles across Niagara County if you head for Niagara Falls and eighteen miles if you head for Pendleton.

NYS Office of Parks & Recreation

Fort Niagara is a great stone bastion begun by the French in 1679.

A long stone ridge stood between Lockport and Lake Erie, blocking a level passageway. A cut over three miles long using hand tools and explosives had to be opened — quite an achievement in its day. The original Great Cut of Clinton's Ditch has been enlarged several times; today the Erie Barge Canal passes through the exact location chosen in 1821.

The boat excursions through the locks at Lockport also extend into the Great Cut. This is the best way to experience it. By bicycle, look for a vantage point to peer into the cut as you cycle along. The ugly piles (spoil) of stone and dirt towering as high as seventy feet are rubble extracted continuously for almost two centuries.

A Special Note on Visiting Canada

The Niagara Peninsula of Ontario is a wonderful place for cycling. Cross over one of the three Niagara Falls bridges to Canada. Each of the three bridges between the United States and Canada is bicycle-friendly and offers different perspectives on the falls, the whirlpools, and river below. In Queenston, Ontario, you can get the Canadian version of the War of 1812.

Legislation in 2004 has stiffened identification requirements. If you intend to cross the border, be sure to bring along a photo ID and before long, you will need a passport.

Less than twenty miles from the Niagara River lies the "granddaddy" of canals in this region — the Welland Canal. This is not a barge canal designed for small craft, but a full-fledged ship canal, part of the Saint Lawrence Seaway system. Much of the Welland Canal is accessible to cyclists. The Welland Canal dates back to 1829, was highly successful and enlarged many times – resulting in the full-size ship canal you see in operation today. Many of the historical wooden and stone locks can still be seen in the canal corridor. Today, seven giant concrete locks (859 feet by 80 feet) raise ships the 326-foot height of Niagara Falls. Remember, the total lift of the Panama Canal is just eighty-five feet.

If you are going to bicycle in the Niagara Region of Canada you should obtain the Regional Niagara Bicycling Map. One of the best bike maps I've seen, it is made and distributed by the Regional Niagara Bicycling Committee.

Chapter 21

Erie County

*Heading southwest on the Canalway Trail out of Niagara County,
you'll enter Erie County in the town of Amherst. The riding is a
pleasant and picturesque as both the original Erie Canal and the
barge canal use Tonawanda Creek. Nearly all of the Erie Canal
between Amherst and Buffalo is closely paralleled by the recently
improved Canalway Trail. Most of the trail is paved with a few
small gaps and stone-dust segments. It is quite scenic, well-signed
and easy to follow, and keeps you close alongside the canal.
It is ten miles to the mouth of the Tonawanda Creek
(the barge canal) at the Niagara River.*

You will come to North Tonawanda and Tonawanda — two communities with a rich canal heritage. The paved Riverwalk trail starts at the barge canal in Tonawanda and goes to downtown Buffalo.

As you ride the Riverwalk, note the strong current in the Niagara River. The river, really a strait, is a major water link between Lakes Erie and Ontario as well as an international boundary between Canada and the United States.

Cycling along Riverwalk, you'll go right by the federal lock, which guards the western entrance to the barge canal. This lock adjusts for wind-driven changes in the level of Lake Erie. You won't be able to see the old Erie Canal; it is buried beneath the adjacent interstate highway.

In Buffalo, where the canal joins the waters of Lake Erie, stop for a moment and reflect on the achievement that the Erie Canal represents. New York State, emerging from more than a century of violent warfare, independently built a vast waterway, largely in stone, across a total wilderness. New York had sought help from the federal government; President Jefferson was said to have remarked:

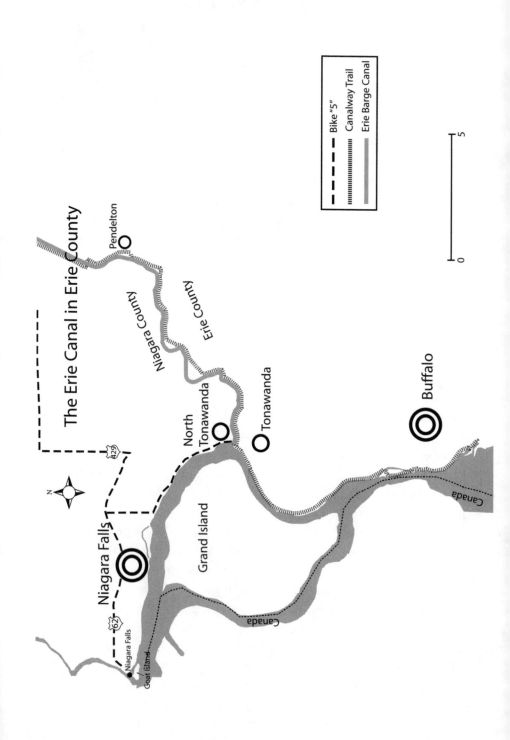

The Erie Canal in Erie County

Pendelton

Niagara County

Erie County

North
Tonawanda

Tonawanda

Buffalo

Grand Island

Canada

Canada

Niagara Falls

Niagara Falls

Goat Island

429

62

N

- - - Bike "5"
||||||| Canalway Trail
━━━ Erie Barge Canal

5

0

The Riverwalk runs along the Niagara River.

"It is a splendid project and may be executed in a century hence....
but it is little short of madness to think of it in this day."

In the 20th century, the state, now truly the Empire State (due in no small part to the Erie Canal), took it upon itself to enlarge that historic waterway at the same time that the federal government was constructing the Panama Canal. The Erie Barge Canal is ten times longer than the Panama and has many more structures, some of which are the largest of their kind ever built. While no longer important in the movement of goods, the Erie has reemerged as a unique and historic recreational resource, unparalleled in America. Maybe its heyday is yet to come.

As you come to downtown Buffalo, you'll cycle beneath the giant International Railway Bridge and the Peace Bridge. The International Railway Bridge celebrated its 125th birthday in 1998. Following Riverwalk, you'll come onto Squaw Island. At its southern tip is a truly unique ride opportunity. The breakwater (or "mole") that shelters the riverfront from the fierce currents of the Niagara is open for cyclists, walkers, and fishermen. Ride out on it. It extends a little over a mile. You'll have the mighty Niagara on one side, and the canal on the other. It is like cycling at sea. You'll go beneath the giant Peace Bridge which deserves special mention as its name is no accident.

The Peace Bridge commemorates the century of peace that the New York and Canadian border shared at the time the bridge was opened early in the 20th century. Almost another century of peace has gone by since then. In the history of the world, this is no little thing.

Buffalo is one of my favorite cities. It is a beautiful city with a network of parks laid out by Frederic Law Olmstead. The Lake Erie waterfront is clean and attractive. Buffalo contains great architecture: four homes by Frank Lloyd Wright, Louis Sullivan's first skyscraper, a music hall by Eero Saarinen, and many other gems. It has, in my opinion, Upstate New York's best food — from local favorites like "beef on weck" and "wings" to international cuisines. The Albright-Knox Gallery is a great museum of art in a beautiful park setting. Buffalo enjoys these things today because it was the terminal of the Erie Canal. The canal made Buffalo one of the most important commercial centers of America in the 19th century. If you have the time, Buffalo is worth a visit.

If you are at Waterfront Park, all of downtown is nearby. Buffalo City Hall has an outdoor observation deck on its 28th floor. On a clear day, go and enjoy its commanding panorama and look back on your tour. Buffalo City Hall itself is an architectural gem; it is the largest city hall in America. You can safely cycle Buffalo streets on weekends.

The Pedaling History Bicycle Museum in Orchard Park is worth considering for a side trip. Containing one of the world's largest collections of historic bicycles as well as extensive memorabilia, the museum is about fifteen miles from the Buffalo waterfront. There are reasonably safe on-road routes to get you there by bicycle. Get a map from the Greater Buffalo-Niagara Regional Transportation Council or obtain current information from the Buffalo Bicycle Club. Their contact information is in the Resource Guide.

Finally, as you reach the waterfront in downtown Buffalo, ride out into Waterfront Park. It was twenty-four miles from your start across Erie County in Amherst. Enjoy this pleasant park which was the terminus of the Erie Canal in the 19th century. You might just spot a lake steamer entering the Buffalo River with a load of grain for one of the few still-operating mills. A hundred years ago, this was cargo ultimately destined for the Eastern Seaboard via the Erie Canal; today it is most likely to go by rail. If it is cargo ultimately destined for Europe, it will not stop in Buffalo at all, but traverse the Welland Canal and the Saint Lawrence Seaway.

Travel Tip

Directly across the Peace Bridge are Fort Erie and the Canadian Niagara River Trail. The trail runs thirty-five miles north to Niagara-on-the-Lake, Canada.

Fishing along the Niagara River.

Four Presidents are associated with Buffalo. Millard Fillmore moved here from Cayuga County in 1822. Grover Cleveland moved here in 1855. Both were attracted by the booming economy brought on by the opening of the Erie Canal. Fillmore was Zachary Taylor's Vice President and became president upon Taylor's death in 1850. President-elect Lincoln spoke here on his way from Springfield Illinois to Washington on February 16, 1861. His funeral train stopped here on April 27, 1865 and his coffin was opened and put on display. Grover Cleveland was Erie County Sheriff and was elected Mayor of Buffalo in 1882, Governor of New York in 1883, and President of the United States in 1885.

Buffalo grew so prosperous that it was chosen as the location of the Pan American Exposition, which heralded the new 20th century. This was to be a celebration of the new found power of electricity, which was centered on the hydroelectric power of the Niagara. This stupendous celebration drew President McKinley, who was assassinated here in 1901, and saw the inauguration of Theodore Roosevelt. The inauguration site is worth visiting. There are only five sites, outside Washington, where presidents have taken the Oath of Office. There is much presidential history in Buffalo.

ROCHESTER

AND

ALBANY.

Red Bird Line of Packets,

In connection with Rail Road from Niagara
Falls to Lockport.

1843.  1843.

12 *hours ahead of the Lake Ontario Route!*

The Cars leave the Falls every day at 2 o'clock, P. M. for
Lockport, where passengers will take one of the following new

Packet Boats 100 Feet Long.

THE EMPIRE!

Capt. D. H. Bromley,

THE ROCHESTER

Capt. J. H. Warren,

and arrive in Rochester the next morning at 6 o'clock, and can
take the 8 o'clock train of Cars or Packet Boats for Syracuse and
Albany, and arrive in Albany the same night.

☞ Passengers by this route will pass through a delightful country, and
will have an opportunity of viewing Queenston Heights, Brock's Monument,
the Tuscarora Indian Village, the combined Locks at Lockport, 3 hours at
Rochester, and pass through the delightful country from Rochester to Utica
by daylight.

N. B.---These two new Packets are 100 feet long, and are built
on an entire new plan, with

Ladies' & Gentlemen's Saloons,

and with Ventilators in the decks, and for room and accommoda
tions for sleeping they surpass any thing ever put on the Canal.

For Passage apply at Railroad and Packet Office, Niagara Falls.

September, 1843.   T. CLARK,
                            J. J. STATIA, } Agents

Resource Guide

Map Resources

It is a challenge to hunt down good local maps, but there is a wide selection of printed maps and online maps available. This Resource Guide will identify the best sources of good bike maps — all are excellent and most are free.

Statewide — On-Road Maps

The New York State Department of Transportation has signed several on-road bike routes. Most important are: Bike "5" which is your guide to the Erie Canal, Bike "9" which is your guide to the Champlain Canal, and Bike "17" which crosses the Southern Tier of New York, along the Pennsylvania border and ties together the southern ends of the Chenango Canal, Chemung Canal, and Genesee Valley (Canal) Trail. NYSDOT has three excellent free maps of these three bike routes which are available at: www.dot.state.ny.us/pubtrans/bphome.html. Click on "Bicycle maps." NYSDOT has begun to sign a number of additional bike routes including Bike "11" and Bike "19" and as these are completed, information will become available at the above website.

Statewide — Off-Road Canal Trails

The New York State Canal Corporation operates the four canal divisions still in service in New York State (Erie, Champlain, Cayuga-Seneca, and Oswego). The Canal Corporation is funding and overseeing the development of the off-road Canalway Trail segments along these four canals. For the 500 miles of operating canal, these are the most comprehensive off-road canal-trail oriented maps that are available. The map is free. Go to: http://www.canals.state.ny.us/exvac/trail/index.html

In addition, the Canal Corporation has published two helpful "Inn-to-Inn" brochures. One covers the Erie Canal in Albany, Schenectady and Montgomery counties while the other covers the Erie Canal between Palmyra and Lockport.

The Canal Corporation has also sponsored a detailed trail guide to the Erie Canal. This is available through Parks & Trails New York (www.ptny.org). Their excellent guidebook titled *Cycling The Erie Canal* has a wealth of information and detailed maps of on-road and off-road routes along the Erie Canal.

Finally, you can find a lot of useful boating information at this website which can be very helpful if you are arriving by boat or would like to take a boat cruise along the canals.

Statewide — Finding Local Bike Clubs

The New York Bicycling Coalition (NYBC) is a statewide nonprofit bike advocacy organization that maintains the best Web linkage to dozens of local bicycle clubs. Most local bike clubs in New York either have useful bike route information posted on their websites, or have contact points identified to ask for advice. Go to www.nybc.net and click on "Links."

Urban Areas

There are nine Metropolitan Planning Organizations (MPOs) in canal territory: (Buffalo, Rochester, Syracuse, Utica-Rome, Albany-Schenectady-Troy, Elmira, Binghamton, Ithaca, and Glens Falls). Each has a bike guide to their local metropolitan area. As these urban areas are the most difficult areas for a stranger to find the best and safest bicycling routes, these detailed metropolitan maps can be very useful. The general website is: http://nysmpos. org. You'll need to go there first, track down the specific area you are visiting, and then contact the appropriate organization. The website is user-friendly, and this is well worth doing as the localized mapping is excellent. Two examples are:

The Capital District Transportation Committee (CDTC) is the source of the essential off-road Mohawk-Hudson Bikeway map. Useful off-road trail information is also available at other MPO sites.

In addition, several MPOs have excellent maps rating their on-road urban street networks. Perhaps the best is the Greater Rochester Area Bike Map, from the Genesee Transportation Council. The map offers bicycle-safety ratings of all local streets. Go to http://www.gtcmpo.org/. Click on "Maps of The Region"; Click on "On Street Bicycle Ratings."

County Tourism

Every county has valuable tourist information at its website or at a website of a county Chamber of Commerce. Rather than list them all, it is easy to just do a keyword search by typing a county name into your favorite search engine. You will find a lot of useful, current information about local sites-to-see, where to eat or stay, and other useful information. A few New York counties do offer special, useful bicycle-touring information at their websites. The best ones include:

Madison County: www.madisontourism.com. Click on Travel Info, then on Bike Tours. A wonderful list of ten scenic bike tours will come up entitled "The Ridges of Madison County."

Cayuga County: http://co.cayuga.ny.us/parks/trails/index.html. Best source of local off-road trail maps.

Finger Lakes: An excellent guide to on-road cycling in six counties — Cayuga, Ontario, Seneca, Tompkins, Yates, and Wayne counties is available at: http://www.finger-lakes.com/. Enter the site and click on "Biking and Hiking." This is a great 32-page multi-county guide.

Other Useful Map Resources:
Mohawk Towpath Byway: http://www.mohawktowpath.homestead.com/
Seaway Trail: http://www.seawaytrail.com/
AdventureCycling: www.adventurecycling.org
Canadian maps: Welland Canal: www.lock3.com
    Niagara Region Bicycling: www.rnbc.info
    Route Verte: www.routeverte.com
Lake Champlain Bikeways: www.champlainbikeways.org

Transportation Resources

Public transportation can provide you with some options in your travel: you can plan an out-and-back trip, bypass a busy urban area, or just rest some tired legs. Some long-distance and intercity buses will handle bicycles, unboxed, in the baggage compartments. These services stretch all along the Chenango, Oswego, and Cayuga-Seneca Canals. Also, buses will handle bicycles along Bike "17" at the southern-most tips of the Genesee Valley Canal (Olean), the Chemung Canal (Corning and Elmira), the Cayuga Inlet Canal (Ithaca), as well as the D&H Canal. Along the Champlain Canal, there are five boat and ferry options to make your ride more enjoyable, as well as the Adirondack passenger train. The key advice is to contact the provider before you go since bicycle policies vary widely. The good news is that with some homework, you can get some good assistance on your trip.

Intercity Buses

Short Line Bus Company: Short Line (SL) is an intercity bus company with biker-friendly policies. SL operates all across New York's Southern Tier, more or less along "Bike 17" from Olean on the west, through Corning,

Elmira, Ithaca, and Binghamton, and across to Bike "9" at the Hudson River and New York City. This helps tie together the southern tips of the Genesee Canal (Olean), the Chemung Canal (Corning and Elmira), the Cayuga Inlet Canal (Ithaca), the Chenango Canal (Binghamton), and the D&H Canal (several places). They also operate along the old Chenango Canal all the way from Utica to Binghamton. They will accept unboxed bikes, but it is best to contact them in advance. Their website is: http://www.coachusa. com/shortline/. In addition, CoachUSA/Western NY operates from the foot of the Genesee Canal at Olean to the Erie Canal at Buffalo, and has the same bicycle-friendly policies. http://www.coachusa.com/wny

There are other bus companies such as Greyhound and Adirondack Trailways, which closely follow the Erie Canal, that will carry boxed bicycles as baggage, or occasionally accept bikes, unboxed. More and more companies are becoming bicycle-friendly as time unfolds. So check them out if you need help on your trip. Boxed bikes are not convenient for a return trip, but will work for an outbound trip. In that case, box your bike in a disposable box, or a box the bus company will make available to you. Then ride the bus outbound, dispose of the box on arrival, and bicycle back to your start point.

Urban (City) Transit

All of upstate New York's urban transit operators carry bikes on buses. This is a big help in congested urban areas, especially on weekdays when streets can be very busy. Perhaps the most important one for cyclists is "CENTRO," in central New York. In the Syracuse area, CENTRO can move your bike from the Erie Canal trailheads in Camillus and DeWitt to the Erie Canal Museum, downtown. In addition, they offer valuable long-distance services from Syracuse, along the entire Oswego Canal and also along the Cayuga-Seneca Canal. The urban buses have bike racks and the long distance buses accommodate bikes unboxed in the luggage compartment. Contact them for details on exact routes and schedules. In all cases, however, don't just "show up" unexpectedly. It is best to make a contact in advance of your trip. Their website is: www.centro.org.

Boats and Ferries

You might want to take a boat excursion at one of your stops along the way. All of these are beautiful rides. A few will allow you to take your bike along, making a one-way boat ride possible. A few options are:

Canal Cruises

NYCanal.com	http://www.nycanal.com/
Mid Lakes Transportation Company	http://www.midlakesnav.com/
Colonial Belle Tour Boat – Fairport	http://www.colonialbelle.com/
Lockport Locks and Erie Canal Tours	http://www.lockportlocks.com
Champlain Canal Tours	http://www.champlaincanaltours.com/

Ferries

If you are cycling north along the Champlain Canal and Glens Falls Feeder Canal, there are some attractive boat and ferry options. No reservations are needed for any of the ferries, but a reservation should be made to cross Lake George. These are:

Lake George Steamboat Company	www.lakegeorgesteamboat.com
Lake Champlain Ferries	www.ferries.com
Fort Ticonderoga Ferry	www.middlebury.net/tiferry

Trains

Amtrak operates all along the Erie Canal (Buffalo to Albany) and all along the Champlain Canal network (Albany to Montreal). The Adirondack, between Albany and Montreal, has special equipment to handle unboxed bicycles. Along the Erie Canal, you may have to box the bike and check it as luggage. Be sure to contact Amtrak before showing up at a depot at 1-800-872-7245 or www.amtrak.com.

Historical Information Resources

Here are some important sources of information. To supplement the resources provided in this book, merely type a keyword into a Web search engine and you will locate all sorts of detailed information. A search will be the way to find the operating hours of a museum, the schedule for packet boat rides, or the date for a community's canal celebration.

Statewide

New York State Parks (http://www.nysparks.com) This is New York State's official state parks website. Many historical sites and all state parks can be traced through this website. You will find historical information as well as valuable maps and detailed schedules of operation.

NY State Tourism (www.iloveny.com)
This is New York State's official tourism website, with key links to all tourism all across the state. It is truly comprehensive, with information about bicycling, and useful links to tourist, county, and accommodations.

Statewide Canal Information

NYS Canal Society   http://www.canalsnys.org/

National Park Service: http://www.eriecanalway.org

Encyclopedic canal history hosted at University of Rochester: http://www.history.rochester.edu/canal/bib/whitford/old1906/index.htm

Erie Canal

Waterford Harbor Visitors Center: http://town.waterford.ny.us/vistor_center.htm

Cohoes Historical Society: www.timesunion.com/communities/spindlecity

RiverSpark Visitor Center   http://riverspark.org/

Mohawk-Hudson Bikeway: See "MPO" websites above

Mohawk Towpath Byway: See "Map" websites above

Stockade District: http://www.historicstockade.com/

Mohawk Valley: http://mohawkvalleyheritage.com/ and http://www. mohawktowpath.homestead.com/

Fort Stanwix National Park: http://www.nps.gov/fost/

Schoharie Crossing State Park: See New York State Parks website above.

Little Falls: www.littlefallsny.com

Erie Canal Village: www.eriecanalvillage.com

Old Erie Canal State Historic Park: See New York State Parks website above.

Chittenango Landing: www.canalboatmuseum.com

Erie Canal Museum: www.eriecanalmuseum.com

Sims Store/Camillus Park: www.eriecanalcamillus.com

Lockport Canal Museum: No website. Call: 716-431-3140

Champlain Canal

http://www.champlaincanal.net/ and http://www.champlainbikeways.org/

Saratoga National Historical Park: http://www.nps.gov/sara/

Crooked Lake (Seneca-Keuka) Canal

http://www.footprintpress.com/FingerLakes/keuka.htm

Chemung Canal (Catherine Valley Trail)

http://www.cvtfriends.elmirampo.org

Genesee Canal

http://www.fogvg.org/

D&H Canal

Wayne County Historical Society (Pennsylvania): www.waynehistorypa.org

National Park Service D&H Canal Roebling Aqueduct:
   www.nps.gov.upde/index.htm

D&H Canal Museum, High Falls (New York): www.canalmuseum.org

Haudenosaunee

Six Nations: www.iroquois.net (Great "links" page)

Oneida: http://www.oneida-nation.net/ and
   http://oneida-nation.net/shakowi/

Seneca: http://www.sni.org/ and (Ganondagan):
   http://www.ganondagan.org/

Dutch Colonial History

http://newnetherland.org/

British Colonial History

Johnson Hall State Historic Site: See New York State Parks website above.

Fort Johnson: www.oldfortjohnson.org

Herkimer Home: See New York State Parks website above.

Finger Lakes

Montezuma National Wildlife Refuge: http://www.fws.gov/r5mnwr/

Women's History sites: www.nps.gov/wori and www.greatwomen.org

Winery Information: www.visitnewyorkstate.net/winecountry

Buffalo — Bicycle Museum

http://www.pedalinghistory.com/PHmuseum.html

Notes

Notes

Notes

Notes

Selected Books from Vitesse Press

Canoe Racing by Peter Heed (2nd edition) $18.95
The Competitor's Guide to Marathon and Downriver Canoe Racing

Cycling Along The Canals of New York State by Louis Rossi $17.95
Scenic Rides on the Historic Waterways of the Empire State

Bicycle Road Racing by Edward Borysewicz $24.95
Now back in print. This classic is on every serious racer's bookshelf.

Massage For Cyclists by Roger Pozeznik $14.95
Clear advice and excellent photos of massage sequences.

Mountain Biking For Women by Robin Stuart & Cathy Jensen $15.00
Woman to woman advice and instruction from two experienced cyclists.

Bicycle Touring Made Easy by Lise Krieger $16.95
"Rider to Rider" advice on all aspects of bicycle touring.

Fit and Pregnant by Joan Butler $16.00
Advice from a nurse-midwife who is an athlete and mother.

Cycling Health and Physiology by Ed Burke, PH.D. $17.95
Using sports science to improve your riding and racing (2nd edition)

We encourage you to buy our books at a bookstore or sports shop.
You can also order through our secure website at: **www.vitessepress.com.**
When ordering directly from Vitesse, prepayment is required. Please include
the price of the book plus handling ($3.50 for the first book, $1.00 for each
additional book) and 6% sales tax for Vermont addresses.

Telephone: 802-229-4243
Fax: 802-229-6939
Postal Orders:
VITESSE PRESS, PMB 367,
45 State Street, Montpelier, VT 05601-2100

Email: dick@vitessepress.com
Web site: www.vitessepress.com

VITESSE PRESS